AIRLIFE'S A

BOEING 747

CLASSIC

AIRLIFE'S AIRLINERS 11

BOEING 747 CLASSIC

Peter Gilchrist

Airlife
England

First published in the UK in 2000
by Airlife Publishing Ltd

British Library Cataloguing-in-Publication Data
A catalogue record for this book
is available from the British Library

ISBN 1 84037 156 0

Printed in Singapore by Kyodo Printing Co (S'pore) Pte Ltd

Airlife Publishing Ltd

101 Longden Road, Shrewsbury, SY3 9EB, England
E-mail: airlife@airlifebooks.com
Website: www.airlifebooks.com

ACKNOWLEDGEMENTS

Without help from a considerable number of people this book
would never have been written. My particular thanks go to airline pilots Dave Peet and Bob Millichap for their specialised
technical input: to Geoff Harber and Hugh Newell for gener-
ously allowing me to plunder their photographic collections;
and to John Roach and Tony Eastwood for allowing me to
extract and use information from their excellent *Jet Airliner
Production List* — which is updated regularly and published in
book form by The Aviation Hobby Shop at West Drayton,
Middlesex.

The photographs in this book come from a number of
sources, particularly Boeing, the airline operators, and my own
collection. I'd like to thank all those whose photographs are
reproduced in the book.

COVER: Braniff 747-SP27 N603BN.

PREVIOUS PAGE: Malaysian 747-3H6 Combi 9M-MHK.

BELOW: Pan Am's 747-121 N771PA was fitted with a side cargo door during March
1975.

CONTENTS

INTRODUCTION

The fact that the Boeing 747 was developed at all is a remarkable testament to the courage and self-belief of a small group of brilliant engineers, all of whom were willing to risk their hard-won reputations by building an aircraft that was so totally different to anything previously offered to the airlines. Its acceptance for production go-ahead was obviously a committee decision, but this too was a notable example of corporate courage — because many problems lay ahead and there was an enormous amount at stake: had the aircraft not sold in very considerable numbers, the continuation of Boeing itself might have been at risk.

The size of commercial aircraft had been growing steadily since the 1930s, with each new generation adding just enough passenger capacity to keep pace with the growth of available markets: airport facilities had developed at a similar pace. The arrival of jets in the late 1950s accelerated this pattern a little, but the first generation of passenger jets were physically not that much bigger than the final generation of piston-engined airliners. By the mid-1960s this comfortable growth in passenger capacity had generated three so-called 'big jets' in the western world — the typically 147-seat (mixed class) Boeing 707-320; the 132-seat Douglas DC-8-50 series; and the 139-seat Vickers (BAC) Super VC10: all three were in the 330,000lb (150,000kg) maximum take-off weight class. Various models of these three aircraft were carrying almost 90 per cent of all long-range passenger traffic and most of the world's flag-carrying

airlines were operating fleets of at least one — and possibly two — of them. The airline industry was not making a huge amount of money out of its first jets, but most carriers appeared to be reasonably content with the capacity of their aircraft. Then, into this world of manageable growth, came a crazy bunch of engineers from Boeing who wanted to throw away all the established ideas, in favour of doubling almost every number you could think of: to the chief accountants of most airlines this must have been their worst possible nightmare.

Although the theoretical operating profits from a 747-sized airliner were highly seductive, they were only theoretical at that stage. Before any profits could be made at all, a huge investment package would have to be put together to fund not only the most expensive airframes of all time, but also the wide-ranging changes to basic infrastructure that would be needed to make their operations possible. No airline in the world, for example, had passenger steps that were capable of reaching the doors of a 747; or baggage-handling equipment that could

operate on such a heroic scale; the maintenance engineers did not have a single hangar bay that could house the aircraft, or the staging needed to reach the outer limits of its structure; the capacity of toilet-servicing units all over the world would have to be at least doubled. These are just a few indications of the kind of pre-service investment that would be needed by all the major carriers before they could even think about sending a fleet of 450-seat 747s off to distant parts of the world — each carrying with it the company's valuable reputation. Airline managers had to make certain that such a huge aircraft could be unloaded, fuelled, serviced and provisioned smoothly at every airfield it was likely to visit. The existing air transport infrastructure had successfully matured over a long period, but it had reached that position only because it had developed in a controlled fashion — closely coupled to the gradual growth

LEFT: Even the shorter fuselage of the 747-SP shows the massive size difference between the 707 and the new generation of wide-bodied jets.

in aircraft size. The arrival of the 747 on prestige routes was going to massively increase the scale of everything virtually overnight and global changes of this magnitude do not come cheaply.

Most of the major airports of the world would also need a significant amount of investment to accommodate even a small number of 747s. Existing hardstanding areas, terminal buildings and pier layouts were all based on the length, wingspan and turning-circle of the then current generation of jets: in some cases even the pavement weight-bearing strength was already close to its safe limit. The anticipated gradual evolution of aircraft had generally played an important role in the planning of airport facilities, but the impending operational arrival of the 747 suddenly presented a whole new set of problems — the burden of which would depend largely on the commercial success of the aircraft. If relatively few were sold worldwide (which seemed likely at the time) the problems of accommodating them on a small number of specially-modified outer stands would not be too daunting. If on the other hand, the 747 was taken up by the world's airlines in large numbers, new terminal buildings would have to be constructed — each capable of handling the virtually simultaneous arrival or departure of five or six aircraft, with upwards of 2,500 passengers and their baggage on board: an equal number of meet-and-greet visitors might have to be accommodated in the public areas. Customs and immigration facilities at a poorly prepared airport might be inundated and baggage reclaim areas could quickly descend into chaos. All the meet-and-greet bodies might put a huge strain on unchanged airport catering services, car parking arrangements and road systems.

The aircraft themselves would need to be fuelled, cleaned and provisioned on a prodigious scale; new baggage handling equipment would be needed to cope with the higher door sills of the 747 and the sheer volume of material on board; the existing 'cherry-picker' elevated platforms would be inadequate for de-icing operations on such a tall aircraft; and all emergency procedures and equipment would need a careful review and possible upgrading to take account of the size and weight of the aircraft and its vastly increased fuel and passenger capacities. Countless changes would be needed to the airport environment in order to cope with a regular influx of 747s — which was a big worry among potential operators of the aircraft in case some authorities attempted to recover the costs involved by imposing excessive landing and handling fees.

Seen from a distance of 30 years or more, this catalogue of potential problems might appear to be overly dramatic. But back in the late 1960s it was certainly not seen that way. The size and shape of the 747 are now very familiar to most of us and high-capacity wide-bodied jets have become the norm on long-range routes all over the world — but the Seattle giant started it all by knocking on the door of an industry that was ill-prepared for such a huge arrival. It could so easily have been rejected at that time — because Boeing was not simply attempting to sell a new and more-efficient aircraft, it was selling an entirely new concept of aircraft operation, and changing a global industry in the process.

1 EVOLUTION

US Government contracts issued during and immediately after WW2 transformed the averagely-successful Boeing Aircraft Company of the late 1930s into one of the true giants of post-war American aviation history. The seeds of this huge expansion programme were planted by the success of the B-17 *Flying Fortress* bomber (Boeing Model 299) — which was designed in the mid-1930s as a multi-engined, anti-shipping bomber (to protect the US coastline) and was later developed into one of the finest strategic bombers of the war years. This single type of aircraft, in all its various forms, remained in continuous production for the USAAF and RAF from 1938 until 1945: 12,731 were eventually built — 6,981 of them by Boeing itself; 3,000 by the Douglas Aircraft Company at Long Beach and 2,750 at the Burbank works of Lockheed/Vega.

Components and sub-assemblies for the B-17 programme were manufactured by 55 major sub-contractors and nearly 200 individual companies spread all over the USA. This was mass-production on a hitherto unimagined scale, and the constant government pressure to achieve even more factory output taught Boeing a great deal about the management and co-ordination of these multi-faceted contracts.

The B-17 itself was the first four-engined aircraft completed by Boeing — which had previously built a small number of multi-engined types (notably the Model 247 airliner) but had always seemed much happier with the single-engined fighter or trainer concept. The Model 299's technical and performance standards were amazing for its day and the YB-17 development machines set several speed and altitude records during their service-evaluation flights. The Army Air Corps clearly wanted this aircraft in its inventory, but bitter squabbling between the US Army and Navy over who should have the coastal defence role delayed its first production order until 1938 — nearly three years after the prototype's first flight. Despite this unpromising start the B-17 soon became the centre of more activity than Boeing had ever seen before, with wartime production at the Seattle plant alone reaching an amazing peak of 16 aircraft completions every 24-hours.

Out of the early B-17 programme came one of the first four-engined Boeing airliners — the Model 307 *Stratoliner*, which made use of all the dynamic components of the B-17C (wings, power units, tail and landing gear, etc) coupled to an entirely new, larger-diameter fuselage equipped to carry 33 passengers. This was also the first four-engined airliner in America to have a pressurised cabin. The *Stratoliner* (and its four-engined flying-boat contemporary, the Model 314) might have had a much brighter future had it not been for their unfortunate timing: both flew during the latter half of 1938, which was not a good time to invest in international air services. These were fine aircraft and the small numbers that were sold for commercial operation achieved remarkable things during the war — often flying clandestine missions over the hostile Atlantic and Pacific oceans, carrying people and cargo considered vital to the war effort

Using all the combat experience gained from early B-17 operations, Boeing resurrected an existing design-study for a larger, longer-range and pressurised development of the aircraft,

ABOVE: The dynamic components of the B-50 bomber formed the basis of the KC-97 and Stratocruiser models.

LEFT: The prototype of the B-17 bomber was first flown in July 1935.

which was equipped with much more powerful engines and a new tricycle undercarriage. This concept was updated during the war to become the Boeing Model 345 — which later went into USAAF service as the B-29/B-50 *Superfortress* series of bombers. When the XB-29 made its maiden flight during September 1942, it had already attracted orders amounting to nearly 1,700 aircraft.

The B-17 lines were still occupying most of the available production facilities, so new co-production partnerships had to be formed with the Bell and Martin Aircraft companies: these would run in parallel with the existing Douglas and Lockheed/Vega arrangements. Boeing produced the B-29 (or sub-assemblies for it) at Wichita, Renton and Seattle: while the Bell and Martin lines operated from government-owned factories at Marietta, Georgia, and Omaha in Nebraska. By the time the war with Japan ended in August 1945, nearly 3,750 of these impressive and complicated machines had been delivered, with combined production rates (from all sites) having reached nearly 150 aircraft per month. The last B-29 was completed in May 1946, bringing the total production figure up to 3,960: no less than 5,000 advance orders for the aircraft had to be cancelled after the defeat of Japan.

Post-war developments of the same basic dynamics were to keep related types in production well beyond the age of the first jet aircraft. A military transport version of the B-29 (the Boeing Model 367) had been designed only a short time after the bomber itself, but the over-riding pressure for combat aircraft at that time delayed any thoughts of large-scale production until the end of the war. Three prototypes had been ordered as XC-97s in January 1942, but their low-priority status resulted in the aircraft being virtually hand-built in the experimental shop and the first did not fly until 15 November 1944.

The C-97 *Stratofreighter* was related to the B-29 in exactly the same way as the earlier *Stratoliner* was related to the B-17: it used the same wing, powerplants, landing-gear and tail assembly as the bomber, but these were grafted onto a so-called 'double-bubble' fuselage — the upper-lobe of which was 11ft (3.3m) in diameter, while the lower one remained the same as the bomber itself. Outwardly, this combination appeared to have all the aerodynamic sleekness of a Dutch-barn, but the XC-97 was actually extremely fast for a piston-engined transport aircraft — as one of the prototypes demonstrated in January 1945 by carrying a payload of 20,000lb (9,072kg) virtually coast-to-coast (3,323 miles — 5,348km) at an average speed of 383mph (616km/h). This level of performance could not be ignored by the military for long and in June 1945 a batch of ten YC-97s was ordered for service evaluation.

At this point bomber development comes back into the picture, because the B-29 design (on which the C-97 was based) was significantly upgraded towards the end of the war to become the Boeing Model 345-2. Changes to the bomber included a switch to 3,500hp Pratt & Whitney R-4360 Wasp Major engines; a revised and more efficient wing manufactured from stronger and lighter 75-ST aluminium alloys; a 5ft (1.5m) taller fin and rudder assembly (which was also designed to fold sideways for ease of hangarage); and many new or updated flight systems. This aircraft entered service as the B-50A *Superfortress* and most of the upgrade changes were also applied to the C-97 transport and its KC-97 tanker/transport derivatives. The B-50A flew for the first time on 25 June 1947,

ABOVE: The Model 377 Stratocruiser was Boeing's first post-war airliner.

and the first YC-97A (the earliest model to incorporate all the B-50A changes) flew on 28 January 1948. Production of these two aircraft kept Boeing plants busy for several years and helped to soften the blow of all those B-29 cancellations at the end of the war. The B-50 line, fuelled by the first political rumblings of what would become the Cold War, remained open until airframe number 371 was completed in March 1953. C-97 production (most of it generated by the demand for KC-97 tanker/transport variants) continued until number 888 was rolled-out on 18 July 1956.

The first post-war airliner built by Boeing was the Model 377 *Stratocruiser* — which was little more than a civilianised version of the C-97. This aircraft differed externally from its military counterpart by having a full set of upper-deck passenger windows: it also lacked the chin-mounted radar that was fitted to all C-97s. Internally the *Stratocruiser* was said to be the last word in luxury — with accommodation on its two spacious decks for only 100 or so passengers: sleeping berths were generally fitted on longer routes, and a lower-deck lounge was connected to the seating area by a spiral staircase. Trans-oceanic travel was a comparatively rare privilege during the immediate post-war years and airlines had to compete with a traditional and well-established shipping industry: as a result, only 55 of these magnificent airliners were sold before production of the Model 367/377 series ended in the mid-1950s.

During August 1941 (before the Japanese attack on Pearl Harbor), jet-engine technology was gifted to the Americans by a British Government concerned about the possibility of German air raids wiping-out the main source of Allied research. All the plans of a Whittle engine were sent out to Washington, followed by a completed W.1X engine and a team of British engineers: finally, Whittle himself went to America for three months in 1942, to act as an advisor on the project and help set up a parallel research and production programme. The Americans quickly realised the potential of these new power-plants and millions of dollars were poured into their development: out of these co-operative studies came the relatively simple engines that would power some of the most famous aircraft in history.

One of the first requirements to be issued by the US military was that for a jet-powered, medium-range bomber to replace both the B-17 and the B-24. Boeing's immediate response was a series of studies based on a B-29-style wing — but with four General Electric TG-180 (later to become the J35) axial-flow engines, in various configurations both under the wing and buried inside the fuselage. One of these — the Model 432 — was accepted for a $150,000 Phase 1 Study contract in March 1945: the service number allocated to this project was XB-47.

A few months later, the shape of the proposed XB-47 underwent a dramatic change. The results of German research into swept-wing aerodynamics had been discovered by US troops during their advance through Europe. Most of the working papers and several wind-tunnel models were shipped to the United States for urgent assessment — much of it by Boeing engineers, who probably had access to some of the most advanced experimental facilities in the industry at that time. After confirming the accuracy of this work, Seattle incorporated the new ideas into a revised bomber layout — the Model 450 — which was given 30° of wing sweep and (over the next few months) a variety of different powerplant configurations. After several amendments to the original paperwork, the Model 450 — which by now had *six* underslung jet engines — was granted a Phase II (Hardware) contract worth more than $8 million: signed in April 1946, this new document called for two prototypes of a totally transformed aircraft — which had somehow managed to retain the XB-47 designation and was now named *Stratojet* by Boeing.

When the first prototype emerged from the final-assembly building during September 1947, it was clear that the XB-47 was no ordinary aeroplane. Its sleekly futuristic look was redolent of every schoolboy's fantasies about rocket ships and defending the earth from alien invaders: bombers had always been such cumbersome and lumpy objects, but the new jet looked so invitingly slippery and menacing that it might just as well have come from another planet. The aircraft flew for the first time on 17 December 1947 and quickly established a reputation for amazing speed and agility — especially for such a large and heavy machine. The familiar, much hyped coast-to-coast spectacular (so loved by US public-relations men at that time) was achieved in three hours and 46 minutes, representing an average speed of 607mph (977km/h).

The early production of B-47s was concentrated on Boeing's Wichita plant, but the rapid build-up of orders following the outbreak of war in Korea soon found Seattle organising yet another multi-source production effort. Lockheed and Douglas manufacturing plants were brought into the programme in 1951, and sub-assemblies were again spread across dozens of individual suppliers and sub-contractors. By the time B-47 production ended in 1957, no fewer than 1,941 bomber or reconnaissance variants had been completed. Despite being spurred into priority production by the Korean conflict, the B-47 was never actually called into action.

Boeing's next major project was the B-52 *Stratofortress*, which was designed to meet a USAAF requirement for very long-range strategic bombers. At its early gross weight of 420,000lb (190,509kg) this was the heaviest aircraft ever flown and it gave Seattle a lot of experience in the handling of huge primary structures; complex fuel, hydraulic and electrical systems; and other novel features such as multi-truck, steerable undercarriages. The origin of the B-52 has been traced back to a broad specification raised during April 1945 — although the finished article bore little or no direct relationship to the earliest submissions. Initial designs for the so-called 'global-deterrence' mission all incorporated straight wings and either four or six Wright T35 turbo-prop engines: one of these proposals (the Boeing Model 462) was accepted for further study in June 1946 and given the military designation XB-52.

BELOW: The XB-47 Stratojet was a truly remarkable aircraft for its day.

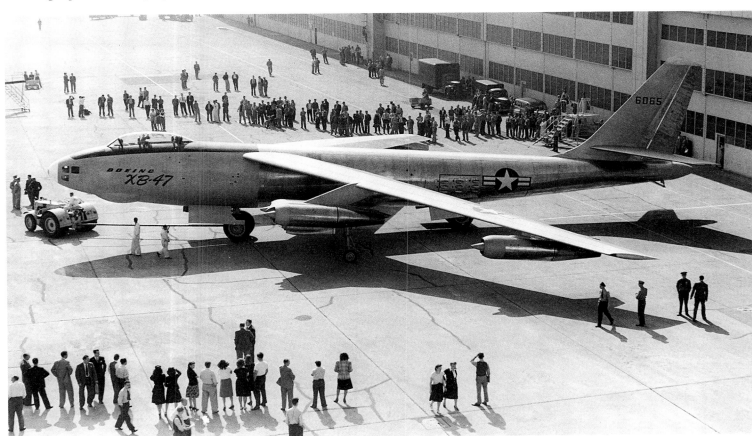

After only a few months of flight-test experience with the smaller XB-47, the recently renamed US Air Force asked Boeing to submit fresh proposals for an XB-52 powered by turbojet engines: this change made good sense in terms of speed, and the planned development of air-refuelling systems — using the KC-97 — was making-mission endurance less of a problem. One of the revised schemes (Model 464-49) followed the layout of the B-47: it had similar sharply-swept wing and tail surfaces, but it was bigger all round and powered by eight 8,700lb (36.66kN) thrust Pratt & Whitney J57-P-3 turbojets, installed in pairs on four wing-mounted pylons.

The first of two B-52 prototypes flew during April 1952 and fully operational examples began to arrive at Strategic Air Command bases during the summer of 1955. These aircraft remained in production for ten years and upgraded models have endured to become some of the all-time classics of American aviation history. All the final-assembly work for the B-52 programme was done at Seattle and Wichita, but virtually the entire aircraft was put together from big sub-assemblies manufactured by outside partner companies. The last of the 744 airframes was completed at Wichita during October 1962.

With several types of high-flying jet aircraft about to enter service (and more to come) Boeing saw a big problem on the horizon if the USAF continued to rely solely on piston-engined tankers. The operational speed and altitude limits of the KC-97 were compatible with late 1940s-style bombers — but the new jets out-performed them in every possible way and this could make fuel-transfer a difficult and possibly dangerous proposition. Various private-venture studies of a jet-powered successor to the KC-97 were undertaken during 1949/50 — some with conventional wings and others using the new swept-wing technologies. Early designs were all based on a virtually unchanged C-97 fuselage and were therefore identified by a continuation of the Model 367 number series.

Very few of these concepts ever saw the light of day, but one that did (briefly) was the Model 367-64 — which married a C-97 fuselage-structure to a moderately-swept wing and sharply-swept tail surfaces. This aircraft was originally designed with two mid-span pylons each carrying a pair of XJ57-P-1 turbojets, but later studies led to the separation of the engines onto four individual pylons. The fuselage was gradually streamlined and changed until it looked nothing like the

ABOVE LEFT: Production of the B-52 Stratofortress gave Boeing a lot of valuable experience in the handling and assembly of very large primary structures.

ABOVE: The unique Model 367-80 was the company-funded forerunner of the entire Boeing jetliner family.

RIGHT: This artist's impression shows the proposed Boeing Model 367-64, with four XP57 turbojets on two wing-mounted pylons.

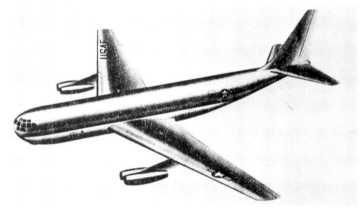

original Model 367 and finally (again as a result of flight-test experience with the XB-47) the wing was made thinner and given a much greater degree of sweep-back.

During April 1952 the main board of Boeing met to consider the future of the new transport. The US Air Force had unexpectedly refused to fund the programme — openly agreeing that a jet tanker/transport should be part of its re-equipment plans, but pleading poverty after spending so much on a wide range of new combat aircraft. This was a big setback to Boeing, but the board was so convinced by the military and civil potential of the aircraft that it finally gave approval to proceed with a single research prototype: $16 million of company money was committed to the project — which by this time had evolved into the Model 367-80.

No one outside the company was aware of it at the time, but the new aircraft had — for several months — been referred to internally as the Model 707. It was clear throughout the later stages of development that any relationship to the Model 367 had been lost long ago: a new model number was obviously appropriate, but in the fiercely competitive world of post-war aircraft development it suited Boeing to hide behind the older (and therefore less interesting) subterfuge-number for as long

ABOVE: Orders for the KC-135 tanker/transport provided an ideal springboard into the world of commercial jets. *Hugh Newell*

as possible. All press comment about the new transport was encouraged to use its Model 367-80 description — right up until the prototype made its first ground appearance at Renton on 15 May 1954. At that stage it became quite obvious that the aircraft was no 'Son of KC-97'. Boeing announced the new model number on roll-out day, and firmly underlined its importance with a reserved civil registration (N70700) on the aircraft.

Thus it was that Boeing entered the brave new world of the commercial jet transport — a world that the company would come to dominate over the following decades with a whole series of brilliantly successful airliners. The board's hunch that US Air Force planners would soon feel the urgent need for a jet tanker/transport was quickly realized: the first order for 29 KC-135A *Stratotanker* and *Stratolifter* models (the military equivalents of the 707) was received only a month after the maiden flight of the 'prototype' Model 367-80. The original order was tiny but it began a story that would continue until more than 800 of these jets were in US military service: most of them were in the tanker/transport configuration, but production totals also included several specialist applications of the same basic airframe.

Military orders provided an ideal foundation for the commercial programme, but the numbers of aircraft involved (and the planned Air Force delivery schedule) forced Boeing to seek US Government approval before it could build airliner versions at the same time as the KC-135s. This was agreed during July

1955, and a few weeks later Pan American Airways ordered six 707-121s: Seattle had taken the first tentative steps along a path that would ultimately lead to yet another 're-invention' of itself — this time from a predominantly military-aircraft supplier to a global manufacturer of virtually every size of jetliner.

The 707 series was stretched, adapted and re-engined several times, and remained in low-level production well into the 1990s. The last commercial models were delivered during the late 1970s, but the basic airframe then reverted back to its military roots and the final few years of production were concentrated on various E-3A and E-6A models: just over 1,000 707-based aircraft were manufactured — these in addition to the 800 or so KC-135 models mentioned earlier.

The 707 was followed into production by the medium-range 727 tri-jet, which again remained in continuous production for 20 years and sold more than 1,800 examples — of two different lengths and several different performance standards. The ubiquitous 737 has undoubtedly outsold every other jet airliner in history — in most cases many times over. With production beginning in 1967, the 737 is probably the most changed and developed aircraft of all time — with modern examples keeping-up with all the best that Airbus Industrie has to offer and still selling in huge numbers.

Sales of these three passenger jets gave Boeing the production experience, customer confidence and financial 'clout' to tackle something as audacious as the 747 programme: no other company could have attempted such an enormous gamble at that time without government backing. The fact that they succeeded so spectacularly well is an extraordinary testimony to the trust built up between the company and its customers.

2 DESIGN

The roots of the 747 programme can be traced back to the convergence of two completely separate strands of Boeing aircraft development — one from the commercial arena and the other from a solely military background. The commercial effort was originally focused on an attempt to stretch the 707 into a truly enormous 279-seater, while the military programme was trying to win a design competition that ultimately led to the Lockheed C-5A transport for the US Air Force. Both studies had a considerable influence on the final size and shape of the 747, but it would be wrong to describe either as a direct predecessor.

On the commercial front, the widespread adoption of jets in the late 1950s had taken everyone in the industry slightly by surprise. These powerful new engines had only recently escaped from the exclusive clutches of the military and their early takeover of the airline world was seen as something of a

BELOW: Most of Boeing's early work on very large aircraft structures was done in an attempt to win the CX-HLS (C-5A) competition.

mixed blessing. They were greeted with wild enthusiasm by highly-polished young marketing executives (who were trained to see everything in terms of exciting new opportunities) and with a degree of nervous trepidation by the wiser counsels of their chief accountants. The scheduled operation of these expensive new aircraft was promoted by the marketing people into some kind of virility symbol among the major airlines, and every carrier worth its corn was persuaded to have them if it wanted to retain a competitive edge within the industry. There was little sign of any long-term strategic planning or forethought behind these decisions: just a mad scramble for early delivery positions. Most airline managements however, would spend their first few years of jet operation on a financial knife-edge, because they were hopelessly ill-prepared for the new problems that lay ahead.

Jet aircraft were extremely costly to buy and operate compared with the final generation of big piston-engined airliners. A number of the more competitive carriers had been virtually

ABOVE: In the absence of any further C-5A work, Douglas decided to stretch the basic DC-8 airframe. *Hugh Newell*

ABOVE AND BELOW RIGHT: Despite being prepared with cargo operations very much in mind, the basic 747 design was eventually developed into a wide range of passenger models: the heavier -200B series was introduced in 1970 and the ultra long-range SP followed in 1975.

forced to dispose of large fleets of comparatively recent (but now prematurely redundant) propeller-driven equipment — all within a year or two of each of each other. This wholesale sell-off quickly created a major glut on the market and led to some really magnificent, low-time aircraft being knocked-out at rock-bottom prices.

As the jets began to take over an increasing number of departure slots, it soon became clear that an over-capacity crisis was looming over many of the airlines' prestige routes. The new aircraft were equipped to carry perhaps twice as many passengers as their immediate predecessors and a given journey could be flown in about half the time: this huge growth in productivity had the effect of a four-fold increase in the number of seats being offered for sale — but extra passengers were simply not available to fill them at that time. Dismally poor load-factors were experienced by virtually every airline during those first few years, even on the so-called barometer routes across the Atlantic. These poor results came at a time when all the carriers needed to boost their profits — not only to pay for the jets themselves, but also to make up for losses incurred during the early replacement of their piston-engined aircraft.

The poor financial state of the industry during the early 1960s was quickly identified as a fares-related issue, but early attempts to resolve the situation displayed an uncharacteristic lack of judgment. IATA had already allowed a premium fare to be charged for jet services (about 15 percent above the rate for slower, propeller-driven aircraft on the same route) but some of the bigger airlines pushed for even higher fares in order to stem the disastrous fall in their revenue. New fares were quickly put into operation, but as the number of high-capacity jet aircraft continued to increase, the available passengers were spread even more thinly — leaving some carriers experiencing load-factors well below 50 percent for the first time. More people were using air transport than ever before, but a significant number of the new passengers were attracted straight into the burgeoning charter market — which, ironically, had been encouraged to grow by the easy availability of cheap and reliable propeller-driven aircraft.

Several years of bad financial results followed, before the scheduled airline industry finally realized that higher fares were not the answer to its falling-revenue problems. The competing charter carriers were often forced by regulatory authorities to operate from unfashionable airports at unfriendly departure times: they were also using outdated, slower and less-comfortable aircraft with minimal cabin services — yet their load-factors were consistently better than the scheduled airlines and profits were improving year by year. The one thing that charter operators could offer (that the scheduled airlines could not) was a significantly lower fare. Charter passengers were required to book their tickets as part of a qualifying group — a club perhaps — but the aircraft were generally full and good profits were being made. The lesson was there for everyone to see.

As soon as scheduled fares began their downward spiral (as a trial at first) in the spring of 1964, the big jets were able to capitalize on their major advantages of speed and comfort: the new fares were still not quite as low as those available on the charter market, but the scheduled carriers had always been able to offer the convenience of travelling from popular airports at civilised times — and without the irritation of awkward booking conditions. Passengers at last began to return to scheduled flights in large numbers and average load-factors of 75-80 percent were achieved for the first time since before the war: jets were operating in near-boom conditions and the race was on to provide more revenue-earning capacity on every flight.

Boeing had watched the fares debate with understandable interest and as soon as the case for cheaper travel had been convincingly proven, a number of design-office doodles began to harden-up into higher-capacity and longer range versions of the 707. The commercial arm of The Douglas Aircraft

Company at Long Beach was conducting the same kind of studies on its rival DC-8 airliner.

The military influence on the 747 meanwhile, had emerged from work done by *'Project Forecast'* — a code-named special investigative committee set up by the US Department of Defense at the end of 1961. The committee's main task was to examine the future operational role of the US Air Force and identify areas of long-term development that would be needed to equip it for the 1970s and beyond. One problem that was highlighted almost immediately was the lack of adequate jet transport aircraft.

More than 460 Boeing KC-135s and C-135s had already been delivered at that time, and the rear-loading Lockheed C-141 *Starlifter* had just been announced as winner of a competition to meet Specific Operational Requirement 182. The new C-141 was a follow-on heavy cargo aircraft powered by Pratt & Whitney TF33 turbofan engines — with deliveries due to begin in 1965.

The main problem with both of these aircraft was their lack of physical size. The US Army (the main customer-

agency for Air Force transport assets) told the *'Forecast'* team that something much bigger was needed: an aircraft that would go beyond the typical 10-12ft (3-3.6m) wide fuselage and carry many of the larger military vehicles — such as an engineers' bulldozer or the M-48 main battle tank. For speed of access the Army also wanted a full-size cargo door at both ends of the main load deck. An expanded version of this wish-list was translated into Operational Requirement CX-4 and issued to industry during October 1962.

In its own way, this single military requirement changed the course of aviation history. It was the first to give us the concept of a wide-bodied jet; and the proposed take-off weight of CX-4 (nearly 600,000lb/272,155kg) resulted in the development of an entirely new breed of jet engine. Both ideas are very familiar to us now, but in the early 1960s such things were beyond the reach of existing technology and almost beyond belief. During November 1963 the CX-4 specification was superseded by an even more ambitious requirement with the military designation

CX-X: this kept to the same general size, weight and timetable as the original, but seemed to drift into the realms of fantasy by adding an incredible mix of advanced technologies — including new materials and structural techniques (for lightness) and a huge, unproven, laminar-flow wing with full boundary-layer control.

All the potential manufacturers took one look at the CX-X papers and agreed that it would not be possible to incorporate boundary-layer control and some of the other technologies into such a large airframe within the time available: these ideas were subsequently dropped in favour of a third, less adventurous requirement, which simply focused on a cavernous cargo compartment with minimum dimensions of 120ft long by 18ft wide and 16ft high (36.5 x 5.4 x 4.8m): straight-through loading and the ability to operate from unprepared-strips were both important elements of the specification, but the use of particular new technologies was left open to offer. This final attempt to find a solution was given the military designation CX-HLS (Cargo

Experimental — Heavy Logistics System). The airframe requirement attracted submissions from Boeing, Douglas and Lockheed, while Pratt & Whitney and General Electric both entered bids for the engine contract.

As we now know, Lockheed and General Electric won the military contest and went on to build 81 C-5As for the US Air Force. The government-funded study programmes leading up to the CX-HLS submissions, provided both the Boeing and Douglas design teams with an ideal springboard into a new generation of commercial jets: Pratt & Whitney also benefited by receiving defence dollars right up to the prototype engine stage. All three companies learned a great deal about the practical difficulties of preparing a very large aircraft structure: about the problems of providing pressurisation and air-conditioning on such a prodigious scale; and about the management of electrical, hydraulic, fuel and pneumatic systems that were bigger and more complicated than anything they had ever tackled before. The C-5A was more than twice the size of any known airliner project: its configuration with a high wing and low load-deck made it quite unsuitable for direct commercial adaptation, but the basic groundwork had all been done at government expense, and at last two big-fan engines were available for anyone with the commercial ambition to use them.

While the work on CX-HLS design submissions was still in progress, Boeing had been talking to the airlines — seeking answers to its quandary over the stretched 707 project. The company's interest in the stretch was announced 'informally'

during May 1964 and the first actual design proposals were floated at the beginning of 1965. Douglas, meanwhile, had been making good progress with the detailed design of its stretched, 60-series DC-8s: production versions of these aircraft (three different models) were finally announced on 5 April 1965, together with the first three fleet-orders from Eastern Airlines, SAS and United.

Ground-clearance during rotation proved to be a particular problem for the stretched 707 and it soon became clear that any changes to the overall length of the aircraft would be technically much more difficult than those encountered with the rival DC-8. Boeing took a long, hard look at all the engineering problems of the project and concluded that a major stretch would only be possible if the entire wing/fuselage centre-section area was re-designed to move the main undercarriage units further aft: this would have taken the programme way beyond a simple modification and into the realms of a virtually new aircraft. The final 707 proposal (the 279-seat 707-820) was engineered along these lines and announced during May 1965. In its high-density layout the -820 would have provided about 100 more seats than the 'standard' 707-320 — but it was a costly machine and received a less than enthusiastic reaction from the airlines. The stretched 707 programme was dropped a few months later: at the time it appeared that Boeing had totally abandoned the high-capacity market, leaving the field clear for Douglas.

During October 1965 it became an open secret in the industry that Seattle had been working on a new model called the 747: virtually no details were released, but it was known that airline opinion had been canvassed on the concept of a 350-seater powered by four of the new 'big-fan' engines. The first official details of the programme were made public at the beginning of 1966. As originally announced, the new 747 was based on a family of three C-97-style 'double-bubble' fuselages — all with the same twin-deck arrangement, but of different lengths to accommodate a maximum of 311, 363 or 433 passengers: the lower deck of each model was split into two separate compartments by the mid-wing centre-section structure and the span of each variant was given as 150ft (45.7m), 155ft (47.2m) and 160ft (48.7m) respectively. The overall dimensions of these first proposals were about 20-25 percent smaller than the 747 as we know it today.

The twin-deck configuration of the 747 was not liked by most airlines: having multiple doors on two different levels, it was seen as unnecessarily complicated to load and service at every turnround, and difficult to evacuate quickly in the event of an emergency. Even Boeing had been giving some further thought to the basic shape and layout of the aircraft. At that time the first supersonic transports were on the drawing boards of both American and European companies and it seemed reasonable to assume that long-range passenger flying would be

ABOVE LEFT: The basic structural elements of the design were tested virtually to destruction in this enormous ground-based rig.

BELOW: B-52 airframes played an important part in the 747 test programme by flying both the JT9D and the CF6-50 engine (seen here) some months in advance of their first flights on the airliner itself.

dominated by these machines within a decade or so, leaving no future for a lumbering heavyweight like the 747. It was therefore decided to optimise the fuselage for cargo operations: the resulting single load-deck would appeal to the airlines more readily in the near-term, and provide the basic airframe with a possible future beyond the age of supersonic passenger jets.

The whole economic philosophy behind the 747 was based on the ability to carry very large passenger loads. The floor area needed to seat and service these numbers would not be possible in a single-deck version of the original fuselage, so a complete re-design was essential. By the time the production aircraft was announced in April 1966, the overall dimensions had increased considerably and the double-bubble fuselage cross-section had gone forever. Instead was a classic cylindrical shape with the cockpit area lifted well above the single load-deck: this military style layout — unique in commercial circles — was designed into the aircraft to allow future cargo versions to have straight-in loading access through an upwards-opening, nose cargo-door.

The new formula had obviously been discussed and agreed with a number of airlines, because a formal announcement of the changes was accompanied by news that Pan American had signed a $500 million contract for 25 aircraft. At the press conference on 13 April 1966, Boeing confirmed that they were planning for a roll-out during October 1968 and flight tests before the end of that year. This was an impressive timetable in its own right, but before construction of any 747s could even begin, the company had to build a brand-new factory: all the existing facilities were simply not big enough to house a single aircraft, let alone a full assembly-line.

3 PRODUCTION

The main board of Boeing, led by chairman Bill Allen, formally launched the 747 programme during early March 1966 but the decision was not made public until 13 April. The launch order from Pan American was backed by 'letters of intent' from Japan Air Lines and Lufthansa, while TWA, Air France, BOAC and Continental had each expressed a strong commitment to the project — although stopping short of an actual order at that stage — about a dozen other carriers had shown a significant interest and all were prepared to sign contracts when the project itself was on a firmer footing.

The principal uncertainty at that time was the balance between anticipated sales of the aircraft and the investment needed to set up the manufacturing programme. Pre-production costs (such as the detailed engineering design, assembly-line tooling, initial materials stocks and construction of the factory itself) had been estimated at $500 million: another $500 million would be needed to fund labour and materials costs for advance component and sub-assembly production; for initial final-assembly line activity; and for the year-long flight test programme leading up to certification and first deliveries.

Compared with earlier commercial programmes the 747 investment represented serious money and none of the funds or guarantees were available from government sources. Building

BELOW: Before any construction work was done, Boeing built this wood and aluminium mock-up of the finished aircraft. This enabled all the detail design problems (such things as cable, pipe and control runs, positioning of access hatches for maintenance, etc) to be worked out in advance. All the basic structural decisions had been taken by this stage.

RIGHT: The big nose-section sub-assembly (known in the factory as Section 41) was prepared by Boeing in these specialised jigs at Everett. The completed Section 41 was then moved into the main assembly hall where it was mated to Section 42 to make up an entire forward fuselage.

LEFT: The main wing-box was manufactured (again by Boeing) in two halves, before being attached to either side of the Goodyear-built wing centre- section box. The built-up centre section of the fuselage (Section 44) was then lowered into place and bolted to the wing: at this stage, all the non-load-bearing parts of the wing (leading and trailing edges, flight controls, etc) and the engine-pylons were fitted.

ABOVE: The combined Sections 41 and 42 (the complete forward fuselage) is transported across the factory on one of the many 30-ton- (27.2mt) capacity overhead cranes in the Everett assembly hall.

RIGHT: The forward fuselage is gently lowered onto two adjustable cradles, before the wing and fuselage centre-section is moved forward to be offered-up to it. Virtually all of the fuselage (except Section 41) was manufactured as 'small', single-curvature panels by Northrop: the individual panels were then transported to Everett by rail, before being assembled to create the giant fuselage sections seen here.

LEFT: The centre-section and wing have now moved forward in preparation for the final join, and the rear fuselage (Section 46) is being lowered into its floor-mounted cradles. Note the two nose sections in the background.

BELOW: By this time the final join 'saddles' are in place, allowing the three major body sections to be bolted together. The extreme aft end of the fuselage (Section 48) and all three elements of the tail are also installed at this time, and the undercarriage is fitted — allowing the completed hull to be moved around the factory more easily.

RIGHT: The engines are among the last of the major components to be fitted. By this stage the aircraft is close to roll-out and simply needs tidying up (note the unfinished wing fillet) before being moved across the road to the paint shop. The apparent break in the fuselage — just forward of upper-deck windows — is actually a dark-coloured sash of protective cloth.

BELOW RIGHT: This overview of one bay of the final-assembly area was taken during April 1982 and shows a pair of Garuda 200-series aircraft nearing completion. The example nearest the camera is on jacks and appears to be undergoing undercarriage function tests, while the other is incomplete and still not fitted with engines.

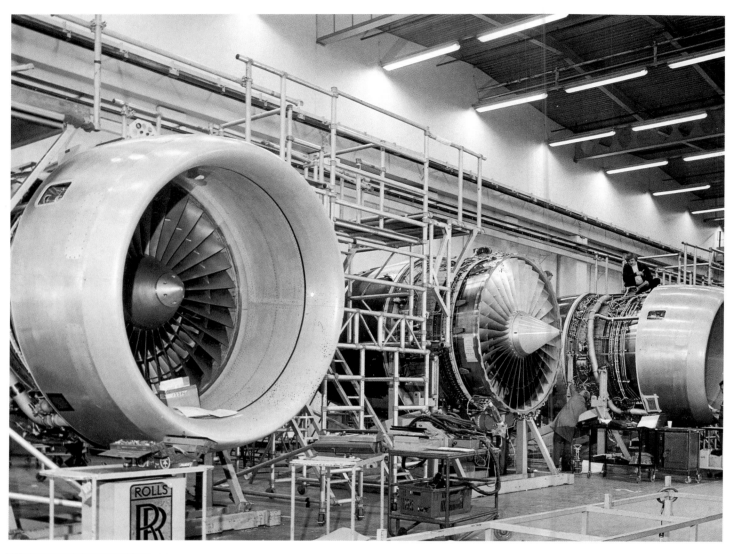

the aircraft was about to become one of the largest industrial undertakings in the world and the billion-dollar investment (or at least the lion's share of it) had to be in place before the final production go-ahead was given. Putting this huge financial package together was a formidable task in its own right and to safeguard itself against any significant shortfall or delay, Boeing arranged a break-clause in the contract with Pan American: this allowed Seattle to pull out of the 747 programme at any time up until 1 August 1966.

The final funding of the programme was achieved on time and with the aid of one of the most imaginative cost and profit-sharing schemes ever devised for the industry. Boeing itself retained complete control of the design-integrity of the aircraft, while extensive financial and engineering links were formed with a wide range of outside 'partner' companies. These partners would effectively handle about 50 percent of the work (by value) and accept a proportional share of the capital risks involved. In return, each partner would receive a continuing share of the profits accrued from aircraft sales.

All the weights, materials, dimensions and standards were laid down by Boeing engineers, but within those constraints all the outside partners were given as much freedom as possible to design and build components and sub-assemblies in their own way. Boeing engineers were responsible for the accurate interface between all outside components and the main hull of the aircraft: company staff would also handle all the final-assembly work at a factory site yet to be chosen.

The major load-bearing part of the wing, its profile, and the profile of the entire nose section were all considered vital to the success of performance guarantees: total control of their preparation was therefore retained in-house. Boeing was also responsible for all sales, marketing, training and customer-support activities, and for the flight-test and certification programme.

While the various partnership agreements were being negotiated, Boeing had been looking at various sites for the construction of a vast new production plant. A large area of vacant land adjoining Snohomish County Airport (the airfield is more usually known by its old US Air Force Base name of *Paine Field*) — close to the city of Everett, in Washington State and about 30 miles (48km) north of Seattle — was selected . A long lease was negotiated and work began on the clearance of nearly 800 acres (323ha) of scrubland during June 1966: building operations started during the late summer of that year. The original main-assembly hall covered nearly 43 acres (17.5ha) — now more than double that — and consisted of three interlinked bays, each 300ft wide by 115ft high and 1,000ft long (91 x 35 x 305m). One of the bays was prepared as an area for sub-

ABOVE LEFT: Rolls-Royce RB.211 engines awaiting delivery.

LEFT: Note the two missing passenger-windows immediately under the cockpit: this gap identifies the aircraft as one of only 13 Convertible (Passenger/Cargo) 747s ever built. The concrete blocks suspended from the inboard engine pylons are needed to maintain the aircraft's centre of gravity until the engines are fitted.

OVERLEAF: Air-to-ground shot of Boeing's main assembly building with a variety of 747s awaiting completion and delivery.

assembly construction and preparation, while the other two were both configured as final-assembly lines — with adequate space on each for a single wing-to-fuselage centre-section join (at the start of the line) and then four increasingly completed airframes. There was also a reception area for airframe components built by outside contractor/partners and delivered via a specially-constructed rail spur, connected to the national railway network. Large sub-assemblies could be moved around the factory and positioned on the assembly-jigs by up to a dozen overhead mobile cranes, each with a capacity of 30 tons (27mt).

The completed Everett plant cost just over $200 million and the first wing sub-assembly personnel moved in during January 1967: at that time total firm orders for the 747 stood at 88 aircraft from 11 different operators. The first main assembly bay was commissioned in late May 1967 and final construction of the first complete airframe began in September that year. Normally a 747 airframe would spend about six-eight weeks on the final-assembly track, but the first aircraft would need a huge amount of individual attention: to allow for this its official roll-out day was scheduled for 30 September 1968.

Major components and sub-assemblies for the original 747 programme in 1968 were supplied by the following:

Boeing, Wichita, KS	Complete nose and cockpit assembly: final-assembly jigs.
Boeing, Auburn, WA	Wing box panels: special production machine-tools.
Boeing, Everett, WA	Final assembly: all ground and flight testing.
Northrop, Hawthorne, CA	Fuselage and flooring panels.
Rohr Corporation, Chula Vista, CA	Engine pylons. Engine pods.
Boeing-Vertol, Philadelphia, NJ	Wing trailing-edge ribs and panels.
Fairchild-Republic, Hagerstown, MD	Trailing-edge flaps and control surfaces.
Rockwell International, Tulsa, OK	Wing leading-edge: fuselage sections.
Goodyear, Phoenix, AZ	Wing centre-section: undercarriage doors.
Aerocal, Torrance, CA	Wing ribs.
Aeronca, Middletown, OH	Flaptrack fairings.
Western Gear Corporation, Everett, WA	Cargo-handling systems.
Pratt & Whitney, Hartford, CT	JT9D engines
Cleveland Pneumatic Tool Co, Cleveland, OH	Undercarriages
Ling-Temco-Vought, Dallas, TX	Rear fuselage, tailplane, fin and rudder

The following suppliers were added later:

General Electric, Cincinnati, OH	CF6 engines.
Rolls-Royce, Derby, England	RB.211 engines.
Shorts, Belfast, N Ireland	RB.211 engine pods: under carriage doors.

4 TECHNICAL SPECIFICATION

Overall Dimensions

	747-100/200/300	747-SP
Wing Span	195ft 8in (59.6m)	195ft 8in (59.6m)
Chord (at root)	54ft 4in (16.5m)	54ft 4in (16.5m)
Chord (at tip)	13ft 4in (4m)	13ft 4in (4m)
Tailplane span	72ft 9in (22.2m)	82ft 9in (25.2m)
Overall length	231ft 10in (70.4m)	184ft 9in (56.3m)
Overall height	63ft 5in (19.3m)	65ft 5in (19.9m)
Wheelbase	89ft 5in (27.2m)	57ft 4in (17.4m)
Track	36ft 3in (11.06m)	36ft 1in (11m)
Overall turn radius	146ft (44.5m)	107ft (32.6m)

Internal Dimensions

	747-100/200/300	747-SP
Main deck length	187ft (56.9m)	138ft 8in (42.3m)
Maximum width	20ft 1in (6.1m)	20ft 1in (6.1m)
Ceiling height	8ft 4in (2.5m)	8ft 4in (2.5m)
Cabin volume	27,860cu/ft (???)	21,660cu/ft (??)
Passenger-floor area	3,529sq/ft (327.8sq/m)	2,725sq/ft (253.1sq/m)

Wing Characteristics (All Classic models)

Total area	5,500 sq/ft (510.9sq/m)
Sweep (quarter chord)	37.5°
Aspect ratio	6.96
Angle of incidence	2°

Usable fuel (US/gal)

	100-series	200-series	SP
Centre wing tank	13,200	17,164	13,200
Inner wing (tanks 2 + 3)	25,092	25,092	25,092
Outer wing (tanks 1 + 4)	8,964	8,964	8,964
Reserve tanks (outboard)	1,048	1,048	2,624
Totals (US/gal)	48,304	52,268	49,880
Totals (litres)	119,445	134,452	127,462

Weight and Performance Summary

During nearly 23 years of continuous development and production, the capabilities of the Classic 747 have improved almost beyond recognition. A really full understanding of the various weight and performance figures for all the different models, their optional-equipment standards and the many powerplant choices, would occupy several volumes of this size. The following figures are therefore simplified and condensed to give just a flavour of what has been achieved over the years.

Basic Operating Weight

Now known in the industry as *Dry Operating Mass*, this is the basic weight of the airframe itself, furnished, equipped and crewed for normal flight operations, but excluding the weight of usable fuel and payload. These are typical basic operating weights for each standard model (without any of the available options).

747-100B	378,000lb (171,640kg)
747-200B	381,000lb (172,820kg)
747-200F	342,000lb (155,130kg)
747-200C (passenger)	391,000lb (177,355kg)
747-200C (cargo)	362,000lb (164,200kg)

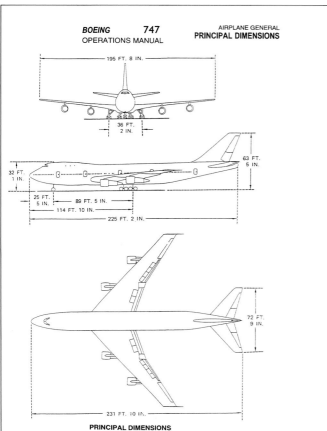

LEFT: Taken from the Boeing *Flight Operations Manual,* this page illustrates the principal dimensions of the original 747.

BELOW: By comparison, this sales-brochure drawing shows the internal layout of the same early aircraft.

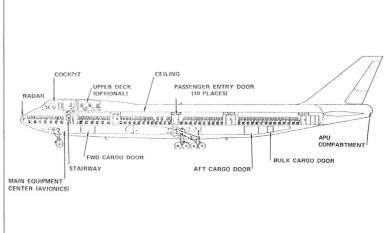

747-SR	359,000lb (162,840kg)
747-200M (Combi)	380,000lb (172,365kg)
747-SP	326,000lb (147,870kg)
747-300	383,900lb (174,134kg)
747-300M (Combi)	387,100lb (175,585kg)

Zero Fuel Weight

Now called *Zero Fuel Mass,* this is the Basic Operating Weight of the airframe, plus the weight of the entire payload: the margin between the ZFW and the MTOW (see below) tells the pilot how much fuel he can carry for that particular sector. The following figures represent the maximum ZFWs for individual 747 models.

747-100B	526,500lb (238,815kg)
747-200B	526,500lb (238,815kg)
747-200F	590,000lb (267,620kg)
747-200C (passenger)	590,000lb (267,620kg)
747-200C (cargo)	590,000lb (267,620kg)
747-SR	475,000lb (215,455kg)
747-200M (Combi)	545,000lb (247,205kg)
747-SP	410,000lb (185,973kg)
747-300	535,000lb (242,670kg)
747-300M (Combi)	565,000lb (256,280kg)

Maximum Take-Off Weight

Determined by structural and aerodynamic testing, the MTOW (now called *Maximum Take Off Mass*) is certificated by appropriate regulatory bodies and must not be exceeded at any time. This weight is largely (though not entirely) dictated by the total installed thrust. The details overleaf list a representative selection of powerplants known to have been used on the Classic 747: the figures show the take-off thrust available from each of these engines, together with the MTOWs (in both pounds and kilograms) most closely associated with each engine option.

Powerplant	Take-off thrust	MTOW
JT9D-3	43,500lb	710,000lb (322,049kg)
JT9D-3AW (water)	45,000lb	735,000lb (333,389kg)
JT9D-7A	46,950lb	750,000lb (340,192kg)
JT9D-7W (water)	47,900lb	775,000lb (351,532kg)
JT9D-7AW (water)	48,570lb	785,000lb (356,068kg)
JT9D-7J	50,000lb	805,000lb (365,140kg)
JT9D-7Q + 70A	53,000lb	833,000lb (377,840kg)
JT9D-7Q1 + 7R4G2	54,500lb	833,000lb (377,840kg)
JT9D-7R4	56,000lb	833,000lb (377,840kg)
F103-GE-100	52,500lb	800,000lb (362,872kg)
CF6-50E/E1/E2	52,500lb	833,000lb (377,840kg)
CF6-45A2 (de-rated)	46,500lb	660,000lb (299,369kg)
CF6-45B (de-rated)	46,500lb	660,000lb (299,369kg)
RB211-524B	50,000lb	800,000lb (362,872kg)
RB211-524B2	50,100lb	820,000lb (371,944kg)
RB211-524C2	51,600lb	833,000lb (377,840kg)
RB211-524D4	53,110lb	833,000lb (377,840kg)
RB211-524D4 (de-rated)	51,600lb	700,000lb (317,520kg)

Ramp Weight

The Maximum Take Off Weight is applicable at the start of the take-off roll. The Ramp Weight (now more commonly called the *Taxying Mass*) represents an additional allowance to accommodate the fuel used to taxi from the airport gate to the runway. In all cases, add a maximum of 3,000lb (1,360kg) to the MTOW figures listed above.

Typical field length for take-off at 833,000lb (377,840kg)

ISA at sea level	10,500ft	3,200m
ISA + 20°C at sea level	12,000ft	3,657m

Maximum Landing Weight

The certificated Maximum Landing Weight (now called the *Max Landing Mass*) is generally dictated by the optional strengthening of wing centre-section and undercarriage structures: it varies within model numbers, but the following are typical.

747-100B	564,000lb (255,830kg)
747-200B	564,000lb (255,830kg)
747-200F	630,000lb (285,770kg)
747-200C	630,000lb (285,770kg)
747-SR	505,000lb (229,065kg)
747-200M (Combi)	630,000lb (285,770kg)
747-SP	450,000lb (204,120kg)
747-300	574,000lb (260,360kg)
747-300M (Combi)	630,000lb (285,770kg)

Typical landing distances at these weights (ISA +20° at sea level)

450,000lb (204,120kg)	5,250ft (1,600m)
505,000lb (229,065kg)	5,750ft (1,750m)
564,000lb (255,830kg)	6,150ft (1,870m)
574,000lb (260,360kg)	6,275ft (1,910m)
630,000lb (285,770kg)	6,950ft (2,100m)

Typical Speed, Altitude and Range Performance.

Take-off safety speed (V^2)
173–178kt (320–329km/hr) at MTOW depending on model (747-SP = 160kt/296km/hr)

Initial cruise altitude
36,300ft (11,065m) after 700,000lb take-off
34,000ft (10,365m) after 735,000lb take-off
32,700ft (9,970m) after 800,000lb take-off
32,300ft (9,845m) after 833,000lb take-off

Maximum cruise altitude
45,000ft (13,715m) after burning off fuel

Maximum cruise speed
507kt (939km/hr) at 35,000ft (10,670m)
(747-SP = 505kt (935km/hr) at 37,000ft (11,200m))

Long-range cruise speed
486kt (900km/hr) at 35,000ft (10,670m)
(747-SP = 489kt (905km/hr) at 37,000ft (11,200m))

The range of each aircraft depends mainly on the balance between fuel and payload: different engines can also have a significant effect, as can various optional fuel tank arrangements. The following figures represent design values for a 'standard' aircraft, carrying either maximum payload or maximum fuel.

Model	Maximum payload	Maximum fuel
747-100B	4,280nm (7,930km)	6,980nm (12,930km)
747-200B	5,820nm (10,780km)	7,150nm (13,240km)
747-200F	4,450nm (8,240km)	7,480nm (13,850km)
747-200C	4,450nm (8,240km)	7,480nm (13,850km)
747-SP	6,610nm (12,240km)	8,180nm (15,150km)
747-300	5,680nm (10,520km)	7,310nm (13,540km)

The landing speed of an aircraft varies with its touchdown weight but typical book values for 747s at Max Landing Weight are as follows.

747-100B/200B	141kt (261km/hr)
747-200F/200C	152kt (282km/hr)
747-300	142kt (263km/hr)
747-SP	137kt (254km/hr)

During the late 1960s Boeing often quoted the virtually unprovable statistic that every 747 airframe consisted of about 4.5 million separate parts. The original purchase price to the airlines of all this material (first announced in late October 1966) was $20-21 million — which at that time was the equivalent of £7–7.5 million. The parts-count, cost and sheer physical enormity of the aircraft gave an impression of great complexity compared with existing airliners — but in fact only the scale of the 747 made it significantly different to the earlier 707 series.

STRUCTURE

The original stress calculations assumed an airframe operating life of 20,000 cycles, which represented 60,000 flying hours over a 20-year period. The basic strength, fatigue and corrosion resistance built into the 747, plus improved maintenance and structural monitoring, has allowed these figures to be surpassed by a considerable margin. The lead example in each category (not necessarily the same aircraft) have now exceeded 35,000 flight cycles, 115,000 flying hours and 32 years in service.

UNDERCARRIAGE

For its time, the undercarriage layout of the 747 was totally unique — with its 16-wheel/four-leg main gear designed to spread the enormous weight of the aircraft as evenly as possible: the inboard (fuselage-mounted) trucks are steerable to minimise tyre scrubbing and surface damage while negotiating tight turns. The twin-wheel nose gear and inboard main gear both retract forward, but the wing-mounted (outer) main gear units retract inwards with a large angular rotation of the wheel truck. All 16 main wheels are equipped with anti-skid brake units.

ABOVE RIGHT: More from the *Operations Manual*, this shows the kind of turning performance a pilot can expect in favourable conditions. Note the steerable inboard main-gear units.

RIGHT: This Cathay aircraft shows the characteristic 53° tilt of the outboard main-gear units.

BELOW: The wide track of the 747 undercarriage is well illustrated by this shot of a Varig aircraft being made ready for delivery.

LEFT: The tail of a 747 is as tall as a four-storey building.

ABOVE AND RIGHT: The General Electric CF6 (above) and Rolls-Royce RB211 engines were added to the 747 programme in 1973 and 1976 respectively.

ABOVE: Iran Air has been operating JT9D-powered SPs since 1976.

LEFT AND BELOW LEFT: At 56,000lb (249kN) thrust, the 7-series JT9D engines allowed the Max Take-off weight of 747 Classic to reach 833,000lb (377,842kg). Here the engine is posed for a typical publicity shot, before being installed in a representative nacelle for testing.

BELOW: The Rolls-Royce RB211 differed from its JT9D and CF6 rivals, principally by introducing a three-shaft layout to wide-fan engines.

RIGHT: An RB211 nacelle can generally be recognised on the aircraft because the hot and cold airflows are mixed much further aft — avoiding the typical 'bullet-tailed' appearance of the two American engines. Compare this photo with that of the JT9D on its test stand (opposite).

main wing box and support the engines at two points. This caused big problems during the first few months of 747 operations, when it was discovered that the JT9D engine casings were developing a slight ovality at high power settings, causing the rotating parts of the engine to rub on the static casing. This took several months and millions of dollars to sort out, and delayed delivery of about 40 completed aircraft.

FUEL SYSTEM

The system capacity varies slightly depending on the model in question (and to some degree on the type of engine being used). The sealed wing-box of a 'typical' early 747 is divided into four major tanks: two inner (wing root) tanks each holding 10,762Imp/gal (48,925l), and two outer tanks with a capacity of 3,863Imp/gal (17,561l) each. The centre-section structure is also sealed to create a fifth tank with a capacity of 10,700 Imp/gal (48,643l). Optional (but generally fitted) reserve tanks in the outer wing-bays can hold an additional 2,248 Imp/gal (10,220l) between them. The typical total fuel capacity is therefore just over 42,000 Imp/gal (190,936l) — about the same as the combined capacities of seven of the biggest articulated road-tankers. Standard pressure-refuelling couplings are under each wing leading-edge (between the engines), but the tanks can also be gravity-fed via overwing filler-caps. An emergency fuel-dumping system is included in the basic specification.

ELECTRICAL SYSTEM

Each main engine drives a single air-cooled 60kVa alternator/generator through a constant-speed drive unit to provide 115/200V three-phase at 400cps: when the main engines are not running, AC power is derived from two similar generators driven by the APU (these are normally rated at 60kVa, but with additional cooling both are capable of 90kVa for a limited period). 28V DC power is obtained from the system's transformer-rectifier units. Standby power is available in DC from a 24V 36A-hr Ni-Cd battery pack, which in turn is coupled to an inverter to provide an AC output for vital flight instruments.

HYDRAULIC SYSTEM

The basic architecture of the 747's hydraulic system was drawn from the highly successful 727 system — which is generally acknowledged to be among the best in the world. On the 747 each engine drives its own pump, which is capable of delivering 37Imp/gal (168 litres) of Skydrol 500A fluid per minute: the system pressure is 3,000lb/sq in. The seamless steel pipes have been made up into long, individually tailored units, in order to minimise the need for connectors and produce as leak-free an environment as possible. The four separate systems all have an air-driven pump as primary back-up. A small electrical pump is also available to ensure adequate braking action while towing operations are in progress.

AIR CONDITIONING SYSTEM

The three separate air-conditioning packs are located beneath the wing/fuselage centre-section. Cold air for the system enters through a trio of fish-tail inlets at the forward end of the

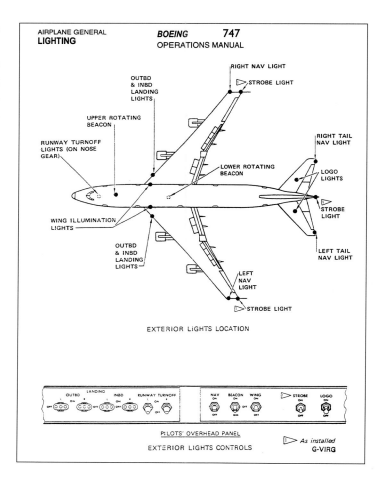

ABOVE: Another page from the *Flight Operations Manual* showing the typical locations (and purpose) of all exterior lights on the airframe. These are controlled from the pilots' overhead panel.

ABOVE AND BELOW RIGHT: Seen here with the captain's seat removed for clarity, the 747 Classic cockpit still seems remarkably small and cluttered compared with the much more modern 747-400 (below). The large flight engineer's station — seen here on the right — is vital to the operation of the aircraft but it occupies more than half the available floor space and accounts for nearly two thirds of the essential switches, lamps and instrumentation: all of this was computerised and condensed into the pilots' overhead panel when the aircraft was upgraded. The mechanical instruments were the best that money could buy when the 747 was a new design, but long-term maintenance of the system needed expensive watch-makers' skills — and something had to change. A number of airlines (KLM for example) are now converting their 747 Classic cockpits to an electronic display-screen standard similar to (though not exactly the same as) the 747-400.

big centre-section fairing: hot air for the heat-exchanger is tapped directly from the low-pressure end of the engine compressor stages. Conditioned air circulates through the cabin from high level to low, and then exits via floor-level vents into the underfloor cargo holds: from there it moves on to cool the electrical and equipment bay, before finally leaving the aircraft via a pair of outflow valves in the lower fuselage.

FLIGHTDECK

Compared to the modern 400-series cockpit, the original Classic version looks surprisingly cramped and cluttered. All 747s until the late 1980s were designed and equipped for three-crew operation and the Flight Engineer's station was a considerable obstruction in the fairly small flight-deck area.

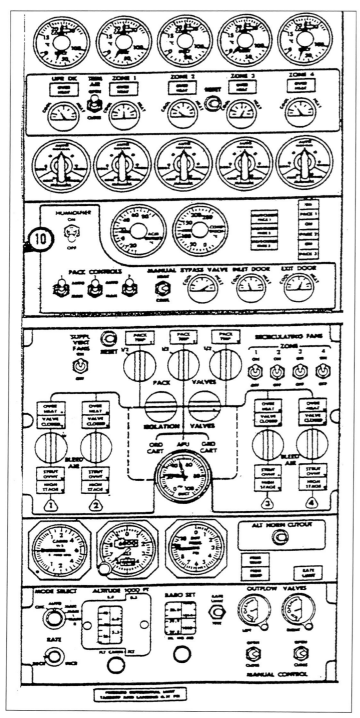

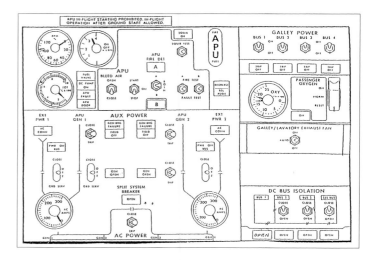

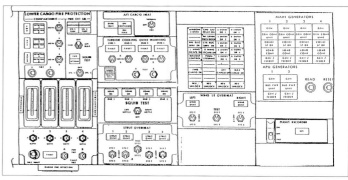

OPPOSITE PAGE:

ABOVE RIGHT AND RIGHT: When the 747 first entered service, most airlines used the upper deck solely as a lounge — enabling first-class passengers to relax during a long flight, but having no seats that were stressed for take-off or landing.

FAR RIGHT: Eventually more windows, fully-stressed seats and emergency exits were provided for the upper deck cabin, enabling the area to be used for more first-class passengers.

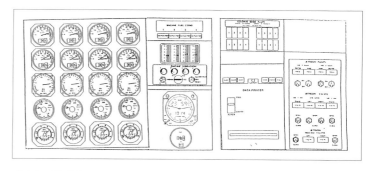

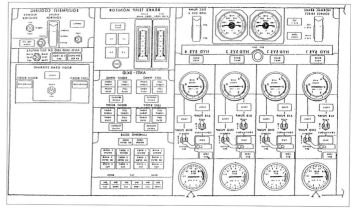

ABOVE: Normally mounted centrally on the flight engineer's console, this panel contains all the controls and indicators for the five-zone air-conditioning system.

TOP RIGHT: The auxiliary power-management panel allows the Flight Engineer to control external (ground power) or internal (APU) sources and monitor their performance: note also the APU Fire panel and the Passenger Oxygen controls.

ABOVE RIGHT: Fire protection and equipment overheat indicators and controls are centralised on a single panel: note also the caution/advisory light panel (top right).

CENTRE RIGHT: This panel contains the engineer's duplication of the pilots' five-parameter engine instruments; fuel heater switches; additional engine-vibration indicators; an accurate clock and controls for the fuel jettison system.

RIGHT: This panel is used to monitor and control the four separate hydraulic systems, plus the complex undercarriage and its anciliary systems (braking, anti-skid system and body-gear steering).

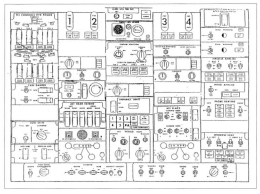

By today's standards the cockpit equipment might be considered fairly basic, but the aircraft did have some of the earliest satellite-communications systems; a basic automatic-landing set-up and — perhaps the most exciting of all — a duplicated Delco Carousel IV inertial navigation system (INS). This was a direct descendant of the system used to take Apollo missions to the

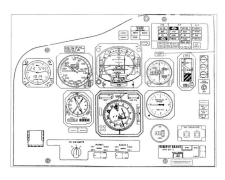

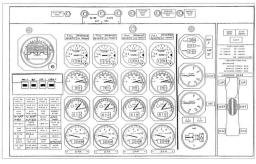

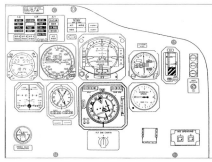

Moon and back, and its inclusion on the 747 allowed the aircraft to become the first to be certificated to fly anywhere without a specialist navigator on board.

PASSENGER CABINS

The internal arrangement of the standard 747 has always been divided into five quite distinct zones, identified by the letters A to E from nose to rear: the shorter 747-SP has only four Zones (A to D).

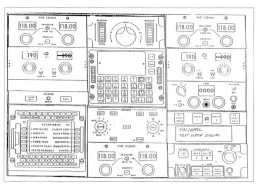

The external door configuration — and the layout of toilets and galleys — have all been used in the past to reinforce this zonal division of the aircraft, but modern cabin designs are more flexible and tend to favour relatively easy-to-move Class-dividers. Seating plans vary widely between the airlines, but provision of adequate emergency exits in the upper deck has resulted in 100 and 200-series aircraft being certificated to carry a maximum of 550 passengers and the bigger 300-series up to 660, all in 10-abreast seating. The 747-SP is currently certificated for 440. The Combi configuration (not available on the SP) uses either Zone-E to carry six cargo containers, or zones-D and E to carry 12. Typical mixed-class passenger loads are 330 with cargo in Zone-E, and only 225 with cargo in zones D and E.

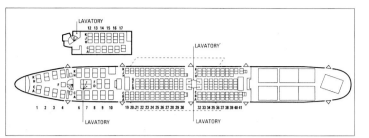
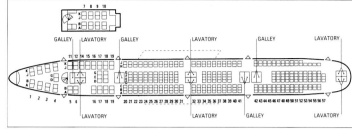
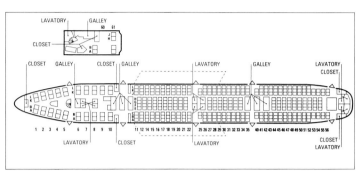
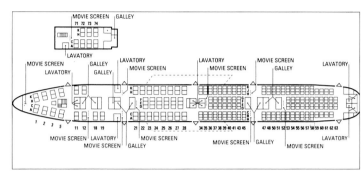
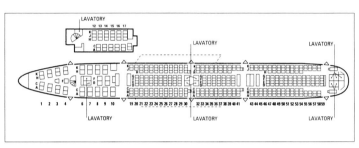
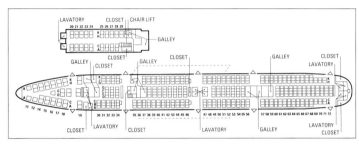
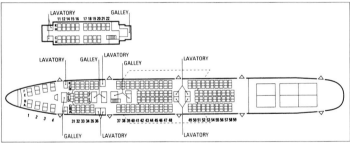
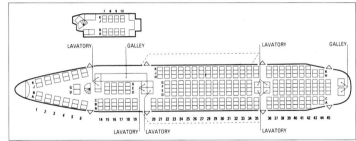

ABOVE LEFT: The flight-deck of the 747 Classic has a fairly conventional arrangement of 'clockwork' instruments: equipment standards vary between airlines, but this general layout remains standard.
Top: the pilots' overhead panel. *Centre:* the two sets of flight instruments and the central engine instruments, together with flap-position indicators; a warning-lamp (CAP) panel, and the undercarriage operating lever. *Bottom:* the centre console (between the pilots) consists primarily of communications equipment and flight-management systems.

ABOVE: Thanks to good planning during the early design phase the 747 is a remarkably flexible aircraft. These floor-plans show some of the seating and cargo layouts that were being used during the late-1990s.
From top to bottom:
Left column: Air Canada 747-200 Combi; Air France 747-100; Air Canada 747-200; Singapore Airlines 747-300 Combi.
Right column: China Airlines 747-200; All Nippon 747-200; Cathay Pacific 747-300; China Airlines 747-SP

LEFT: Alitalia *Economy Class* during the late 1970s.

RIGHT: Pan Am's 1981 *First Class 'Sleeperette'* configuration.

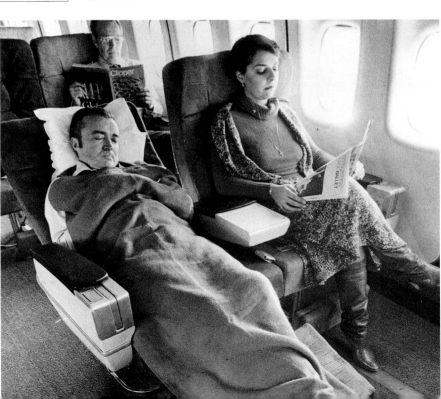

ABOVE: Typical Economy Class seating of the 1970s, looking aft. Note the spiral staircase into the upper deck lounge.

BELOW: Delivery of this RB211-powered 747-338 during January 1985, celebrated 15 years of airline service by various models of the 747.

RIGHT: Without a so-called Air Bridge, passengers have a 30ft (9m) climb to reach the main deck of the aircraft. Shown here is an El Al 747-258C.

FAR LEFT: Decoration of Air India aircraft includes this Rajasthani-style arch around each of the windows.

BOTTOM LEFT: The first batch of 747s delivered to Qantas were powered by Pratt & Whitney engines (as here), but the airline later switched to Rolls-Royce engines and has been using RB211s ever since.

LEFT, BELOW AND BOTTOM: Cargo operations have always been vital to the economic success of the 747. The scissor-lift (left) was one of several portable loading devices designed to be used at the side cargo door, while Lufthansa's vertical hoist was a fixed installation for loading up to 40ft (12m) long intermodal (road/rail) containers through the nose-door of Freighter or Convertible models. The underfloor cargo hold of all 747s (bottom) can take larger loads than the main deck accommodation on most first-generation jet liners.

LEFT: The side cargo door was originally developed as a retrofit to existing passenger aircraft, but it was quickly offered as a production-line option and the new 'Combi' configuration was born.

BELOW: After this successful Lufthansa operation (taking 30 Volkswagens to Hong Kong), several car manufacturers entered long-term charter arrangements with 747 operators. Thousands of cars have now been transported across the world in these cavernous aircraft.

BOTTOM: 747 Freighter cargo door arrangements.

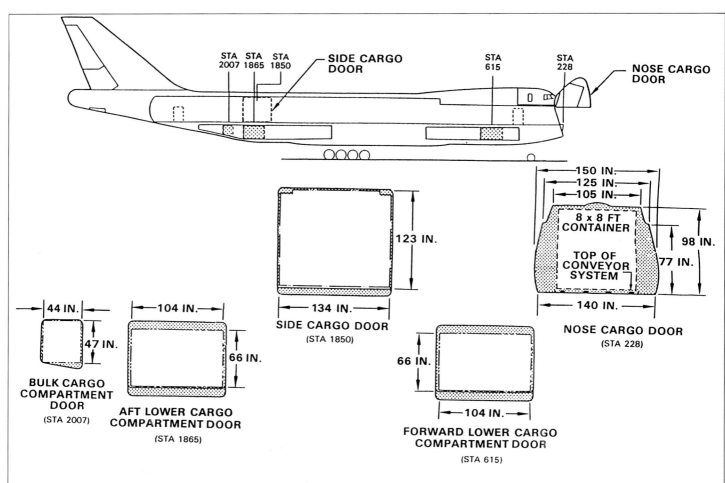

BULK CARGO COMPARTMENT DOOR
(STA 2007)

AFT LOWER CARGO COMPARTMENT DOOR
(STA 1865)

SIDE CARGO DOOR
(STA 1850)

FORWARD LOWER CARGO COMPARTMENT DOOR
(STA 615)

NOSE CARGO DOOR
(STA 228)

ABOVE: The roller-conveyor floor of the 747 cargo aircraft can move awkward-shaped loads in virtually any direction to ensure accurate tie-down positioning. This facility is vital to the successful management of an aircraft's centre-of-gravity.

BELOW: The nose door of this 747-273C (Convertible) is about to close and lock, giving a good illustration of the gap — caused by the need to reinforce the underlying structure there — in what would normally be a continuous line of windows.

THIS PAGE: Three photographs of freighters. Full-time cargo aircraft (designated 747Fs) generally have no passenger windows on the main deck — and only optionally on the upper deck. Only two passenger-style doors are fitted, both on the right-hand side of the fuselage.

5 IN SERVICE

747 PROTOTYPE

First flown: 9 February 1969

The very first 747 was not a 'prototype' in the true sense of the word, but a lead-in production aircraft — built to the same general specification as the 747-21s ordered by launch-customer Pan Am. The first aircraft was unique because its internal arrangements were specially prepared during final assembly to accommodate all the test-equipment and observer-stations needed for the early part of FAA certification trials. Only one aircraft of this configuration was built (Line No.1 — N7470): it was retained by Boeing throughout its life as a test and evaluation machine for new 747 engines, systems, avionics, operational procedures etc. The aircraft was rolled-out from the Everett factory on 30 September 1968, but its first flight was delayed until 9 February 1969 — mainly because of various difficulties with the installation and calibration of all its test systems.

After conducting the first flight and taking part in the initial type-clearances and pre-certification flight-test programme — during which it handled virtually all of the aerodynamic and flutter testing — the aircraft settled into a busy routine of product-development flying. Most of the subsequent changes to the 747 (technical or operational) were in some way routed through this first airframe — starting in early 1970 with a

ABOVE: First flight of the prototype 747 on take-off.

BELOW: BOAC/British Airways retained its JT9D-powered 737-136s for nearly 30 years. G-AWNA arrived March 1970 and finally left Heathrow in 1999. *Hugh Newell*

series of flights designed to certify the basic aircraft for the carriage of a fifth (spare) engine under the port wing. The aircraft was later modified many times to carry out individual equipment test programmes and it eventually conducted engine trials with many different versions of the JT9D, as well as proving the General Electric CF6 for 747 operations.

By 1983 most of the development work on the 747 Classic models had been completed and N7470 was taken out of active service and flown to Las Vegas, where it was parked in the arid desert conditions of Nevada to await a decision regarding its future. In March 1990, after a long period of enforced storage, the aircraft was finally donated by Boeing to the Seattle-based Museum of Flight — where it should have begun a long and honourable retirement. This attempt at 'retirement' did not last long however, because the company leased it back from the Museum during 1991 to conduct one final series of important trials. This time the modifications were centered on the port inner (No.2) engine pylon and its surrounding wing structure: the tests involved flight clearance of two massive engines (the 84,000lb/(373kN) thrust Pratt & Whitney PW4084 and the 90,000lb/(400kN) thrust Rolls-Royce Trent 890) — both of which were destined for the new Boeing 777 airliner.

747-100

First flown: 11 April 1969

The early production 747s were originally delivered with no individual model number: the Boeing type-number was simply followed by a customer code number, so all Pan Am aircraft were referred to as 747-21s; TWA aircraft were 747-31s; and Lufthansa and Air France deliveries were designated 747-30s and 747-28s respectively. This numbering

system continued until the upgraded and more powerful 747B was well into its pre-certification flight-testing: at that stage the 747B (see next entry) was re-numbered to become the 747-200B series and the earlier 'basic' 747 became the 747-100 series (the -100 designation was immediately applied to existing orders and options; to all unfinished aircraft; and then retrospectively to all completed aircraft — so the examples mentioned above became 747-121s, 747-131s, 747-130s and 747-128s, etc).

The initial production run of 'basic' 747s was originally planned around the 41,000lb (182kN) thrust JT9D-1 engine, which would have given a maximum take-off weight (mtow) of 680,000lb (308,443kg). In the event, structural weight problems made this combination of engine and planned weight impossibly uneconomic, so the more powerful JT9D-3 (rated at 43,500lb/193kN) was installed for the first flight and chosen for the initial production batch, allowing the mtow to go up to 710,000lb (322,051kg): later aircraft would have even more power and more weight. A few 747F (Freighter) and 747C (Convertible) versions of the -100 series had been ordered at the 680,000lb (308,443kg) mtow, but when the structural weight problems began to eat into promised payload capacity, all such commitments were either cancelled or converted into additional orders for passenger aircraft.

Some of Pan Am's very early production aircraft were returned to Everett (starting Nov '70) for a series of modifications to rectify in-service faults and to bring them up to a maxi-

mum take-off weight of 735,000lb (333,390kg): JT9D-3AW (W = water injection) engines rated at 45,000lb (176kN) thrust were fitted, and minor changes were made to the doors and passenger cabin, landing gear, flaps and fuel system. Following modification, these aircraft were temporarily referred to by Pan Am (though not by Boeing) as 747As. A total of 167 747-100s were built before the aircraft was superseded by the -200B series.

747B (later known as the 747-200B)
First flown: 11 October 1970
Announced in June 1968 — three months before roll-out of the very first 747 — the upgraded 747B was a successful attempt by Boeing to restore the performance guarantees of the original design. The B-model had the advantage of JT9D-3AW water injection engines, which had been developed by Pratt & Whitney to offer 45,000lb (176kN) of thrust. Certification of the new aircraft was aimed at a maximum take-off weight of 775,000lb (351,534kg) — which at last made Convertible (747C) and Freighter (747F) versions of the basic design a real-

BELOW: This Kuwait Airways 747-269B Combi (9K-ADB, *Al Jaberiya*) was delivered to the airline during August 1978. *Geoff Harber*

RIGHT: The 747-200F freighter is now in widespread use all over the world. This Korean Airlines example (HL7452) is seen taxiing towards its stand at Los Angeles (LAX) Airport. *Geoff Harber*

istic proposition. Boeing engineers had been planning to develop the aircraft along these lines — but not until much later. To achieve this new take-off weight, the wing/fuselage centre-section and undercarriage both had to be strengthened but there were no visible differences between the original 747 (-100) and the upgraded 747B.

During the last few weeks of 1969 the 747B was formally given the new Boeing designation 747-200B, while all the earlier airframes — many of them ordered but not yet built — were re-numbered to become the 747-100 series. The first completed 747B (hull No.88 — a 747-251B for Northwest Orient) was flown as N611US on 11 October 1970. The basic -200 series remained in production for nearly 18 years, during which its optional take-off weight increased to 833,000lb (377,842kg): the last aircraft of this type was built as hull No. 699 — a 747-256B (EC-EEK) for Iberia.

747-200F (Freighter)

First flown: 20 November 1971

This was basically a strengthened 747-200B airframe, but with special modifications for a full-time cargo-carrying role. The first aircraft (No.168/D-ABYE, a 747-230F for Lufthansa) was rolled-out during October 1971 and flew for the first time on 30 November. These aircraft had extra strength built into the undercarriage and wing/fuselage centre-section (to cope with heavier-weight landings) and a much stronger main deck floor; there were no passenger windows on either side of the fuselage and only two passenger-style doors were fitted — both on the left hand side, one at the front and one at the rear. The access stairs to the upper deck were replaced by a retractable ladder. The entire nose-section of the aircraft was hinged just forward of the cockpit and opened upwards to form a straight-in loading-door with access to the main deck (the side cargo door was not introduced on 747s until 1973). The floor of the main deck cargo compartment was equipped with a two-lane, mechanical load-handling system, which allowed heavy freight containers to be brought in through the nose and steered into position before lock-down: a well-trained two-man crew could empty or fill the compartment (with pre-loaded pallets or containers) in about 30 minutes. Both the nose door and the cargo-handling system were electrically powered. The aircraft itself was powered by Pratt & Whitney JT9D-7W engines, which provided 47,900lb (212kN) of thrust (with water/methanol injection). The maximum take-off weight of the first 747-200F was 775,000lb (351,534kg).

Sales of the 747-200F were initially very poor and the second aircraft was not produced until June 1974, when airframe No.242 (N701SW — for Seaboard and Western) was rolled out. The Seaboard and Western aircraft (and most subsequent 747-200Fs) were significantly different from the original freighter design, because in addition to the nose door, they were also fitted with an optional side cargo door (SCD) — which by then had been developed by Boeing to convert existing 747-100 and -200 series airframes into freighters. The new

door allowed 10ft (3m) high containers into the rear fuselage area — something that would not have been possible with just the nose door. The Seaboard aircraft were also fitted with a full set of optional upper-deck passenger windows (and extra emergency exits), which allowed military personnel to be carried on cargo charters for the US Department of Defense.

Production of the 747-200F continued well into the era of the 747-400 and nine out of the last ten Classics built were actually dedicated freighters — all of them fitted with the side cargo door. By the time production came to an end in October 1991, the maximum take-off weight of the 747-200F had been increased to 833,000lb (377,842kg): the final -200 series aircraft to leave Everett was hull No.886 — a 747-281F, destined to serve with Nippon Cargo Airlines as JA8194.

747-200C (Convertible)

First flown: 23 March 1973

These aircraft were fitted with the big nose door of the -200F and virtually a full set of main deck passenger windows. Each airframe was capable of carrying a full load of cargo; a full load of passengers; or a mixed load of cargo and passengers. The only visible difference between the 747-200C and a conventional 747-200B passenger aircraft, is that two windows are missing from each side of the forward fuselage of the Convertible — these being removed to accommodate the massive frames and lock mechanism of the upwards-opening cargo door. The Convertible has the same strengthened floor beams as a dedicated freighter, but the roller-conveyor cargo-handling system has to be installed and

TOP LEFT: This UTA 747-2B3F (F-GPAN) is fitted with a Side Cargo Door (note the sloping rain deflector above the door). The CF6-powered aircraft was delivered during September 1978.

CENTRE LEFT: Convertible (747C) aircraft could be used for passengers or (as here) for cargo. This Iraqi Airways 747-270C was equipped with the on-board loader system, which made it completely independent of ground-based cargo-handling equipment.

LEFT: The first E-4A airframes were not fitted with the big satellite-communications antenna or fuel-receiving equipment in the nose.

RIGHT: The SR version of the 747-100 is externally indistinguishable from the parent aircraft — but it carries many more passengers.

removed every time as part of the lengthy role-conversion process. This is definitely not a 727/737-style QC (Quick Change) aircraft — with the average conversion time being quoted as 20/24hr for a well-trained team of 35 men. The first -200Cs were powered by JT9D-7AW engines, with a thrust-rating of 46,950lb/209kN (dry), or 48,750lb/217kN with water/methanol injection: these provided a maximum take-off weight of 775,000lb (351,534kg).

Only 13 747-200Cs were built, the first three going to World Airways — which used them for passenger flying during the busy summer months and for military cargo contracts during the winter. Most operators followed a similar pattern of summer/winter usage, but the Convertible aircraft was also capable of being used in a mixed traffic role: originally with passengers in the rear compartment and cargo containers up front — hidden from view by a movable cabin divider. The versatility of this model was later improved by provision of the Side Cargo Door (SCD), which allowed freight to be carried in the rear and returned passengers to the front — where they could now enjoy the facilities of the upper deck. The first 747-200Cs fitted with the new side-door were YI-AGN and YI-AGO (Line Nos 287 and 289), which were delivered to Iraqi Airways during the summer of 1976: these two aircraft were also the first to be fitted with the optional on-board loader system, which made them completely independent of all ground-based cargo-handling equipment.

E-4A

First flown: 13 June 1973

During February 1973 the Electronic Systems Division of the United States Air Force ordered two 747-200B airframes for conversion into Advanced Airborne National Command Post (AABNCP) aircraft. These were to be used as long-range, mobile war rooms, to provide continuous (and relatively invulnerable) communication with American nuclear forces at times of dire national emergency. A third aircraft was ordered in July 1973 and a fourth in December 1973 — although these two were not fully funded until FY-74/75: in 1976 it was announced that the total fleet would eventually increase to six aircraft, but such plans have long-since been dropped.

The first two E-4A airframes (73-1676 and 1677) were both powered by 47,900lb (212kN) thrust JT9D-7W engines, but the third (74-0787) was powered by General Electric F103-GE-100s — the 52,500lb (233kN) thrust military equivalent of the CF6-50E. The first aircraft began its flight tests at Everett on 13 June 1973 and was delivered to Andrews AFB (Maryland) during December 1974. The basic mission-equipment fitted to all three E-4As was transferred from three EC-135 (Boeing 707) aircraft, which had previously been allocated the Command Post tasking. The E-4As did not represent a big tactical advantage over the EC-135s, but they did provide a valuable source of operational experience for the later, more ambitious, E-4B programme.

747-SR (Short Range)

First flown: 31 August 1973

The short range version of the 747-100 was developed specially for operations on the inter-island domestic routes of Japan Air Lines. There are no visible differences between this and the baseline -100 series, but the underlying structure has been strengthened to absorb 52,000 take-off/landing cycles over a 20 year life span (more than twice the number expected for a conventional 747). Typical routes flown by these aircraft can include sectors of less than 100 miles (161km), but the average is between 500 and 1,000 miles (805–1,609km). Because journey times are short, passenger comfort is generally sacrificed for high capacity and the SR is usually configured to carry at least 500 people (with minimal galley facilities). The aircraft is used most frequently for one-day business trips: low fuel weight and a typical lack of passenger baggage, means that the average take-off weight is very low (610,000lb/276,691kg). Under these conditions the engines can successfully be de-rated to extend their overhaul lives. The SR has the same fuel capacity as a conventional 747-100, so the aircraft can be used on longer routes if required.

The first 747-SR (JA8117 — an SR46 for Japan Air Lines) made its maiden flight from Everett on 31 August 73: since then a total of 26 aircraft (based on the -100 series airframe) have been supplied — both to Japan Air Lines and All Nippon Airways. The same option was later introduced for the stretched upper deck aircraft, which became the high-capacity 747-300SR (see entry on page 64).

747-100/200SCD (Side Cargo Door)

First flown: January 1974

Although this is not a Boeing production-line designation, the letters SCD frequently appear against 747 entries in books and magazines: some explanation is therefore necessary. During 1973/74 many airlines were having a difficult time trying to fill their 747s with passengers, and some aircraft were being sold-off or put into temporary storage. To ease the burden of these carriers (and to reduce the number of used aircraft being offered for sale) Boeing introduced an 11ft wide by 10½ft (3.3m x 3.2m) high side cargo door for the 747. This would allow the operators of passenger-only aircraft to carry big road/rail freight containers in the rear of the main load deck: it would also introduce a more flexible loading regime to operators of full-time cargo aircraft. The door was offered (with or without windows) as a production-line option, or as a retrofit to existing aircraft. New passenger-carrying models fitted with the SCD during assembly were then called Combis (to represent the combination of passengers and cargo on the same deck) and existing aircraft that were retrofitted with the door simply had the suffix SCD added to their basic designation. During the early days of this option/modification programme, the differentiation between Combi and SCD models was important, but nowadays people loosely describe any passenger-carrying 747 model with the side cargo door as a Combi — which is not strictly correct.

The first aircraft to be modified were two Sabena 747-129s (OO-SGA and OO-SGB) which had been in service since

ABOVE: Alia — Royal Jordanian Airlines — introduced CF6-powered 747-2D3B Combis during the summer of 1977.

ABOVE LEFT: VR-HMF, a 747-200F of Air Hong Kong (which has both nose and side cargo doors), climbs away from Manchester Airport. Note the three windows on the upper deck. *Hugh Newell*

November 1970: these were delivered to Boeing during the 1973/74 winter period and returned to Brussels as 747-129SCDs in time for the 1974 summer season. The modification (or option) has now been undertaken on a very large number of 747s of all series and model numbers, including most 747-200Fs (which already have the big cargo door in the nose).

747-100SF (Special Freighter)
First flown: August 1974
The introduction of the side cargo door spawned several 'new' models of the 747 — all based on the conversion of existing airframes. In addition to the Combi-style mixed traffic version, Boeing converted a number of ordinary -100 series passenger carriers into full-time cargo aircraft. The changes here included strengthening of the entire floor area and its supporting structure; removal of all the passenger facilities (galleys, toilets, upper-deck stairs, etc); blanking-off the passenger-deck windows and sealing all but two of the passenger entry doors. The aircraft was then fitted with a normal side cargo door (without windows) and a full length roller-conveyor cargo-handling system. The engines were also upgraded to the 46,950lb (209kN)

thrust JT9D-7, which increased the maximum take-off weight to 733,000lb (332,483kg), compared to 710,000lb (322,051kg) with the original JT9D-3s.

These conversions were called Special Freighters to separate them from the nose-door equipped 747-200F models. The first aircraft of this type were two ex-American Airlines 747-123s, which were converted during the summer of 1974 and delivered to Flying Tiger Airlines in August and September of that year.

Since then the SF conversion has proved to be an exceptionally popular way of revitalising unwanted passenger 747s — especially as airlines complete large 'roll-over' orders and switch to the more fuel-efficient 747-400 series.

747-200M (Combi)
First flown: 18 November 1974
Although rarely used now, the original Boeing designation for a Combi model was 747-200M (the 'M' suffix apparently indicating Main-deck cargo-carrying capability). All -200 series aircraft that were fitted with the side cargo door as an original production-line option are true 747-200M Combis.

All Combis have a side cargo door (with passenger windows) on the left-hand side of the rear fuselage; a strengthened floor covering Zones D & E of the main cabin; a movable cabin divider (to blank off Zone E or Zones D & E) and a removable roller-conveyor cargo handling system.

The first production aircraft (C-GAGA — a 747-233B Combi for Air Canada) completed its maiden flight on 18 November 1974 and went into service during March 1975. The

versatility of the new configuration quickly led to more sales and the Combi went on to become one of the most popular of all individual Classic (and 747-400) models: by the time Classic production ended in the early 1990s, nearly 70 new aircraft had been delivered.

E-4B

First flown: 29 April 1975

The fourth aircraft of the E-4 series (see E-4A above) was destined from the start to be the first E-4B — powered by General Electric F103-GE-100 engines and equipped with a more advanced mission-equipment package. The E-4B (75-0125) was recognisably different from the earlier E-4As, because the later aircraft was fitted with a flight-refuelling receptacle which changed the profile of the nose, and a roof-mounted fairing to house satellite and SHF communications equipment. The one and only new-build E-4B flew for the first time on 29 April 1975 and was delivered to the US Air Force during August '75.

After delivery, the 'green' airframe was fitted with a special 1,200kVA electrical system (two 150kVA generators on each engine instead of the usual one) and was then handed over to E-Systems Inc of Greenville, Texas, for installation of the high-security battle systems. The completed aircraft flew for the first time on 10 June 1978 and was re-delivered to the US Air Force at Offutt AFB, Nebraska, just before Christmas of 1979.

Following a year of E-4B operational-capability trials and systems refinements, all three of the earlier E-4As were brought up to the same F-103-powered E-4B standard.

747-SP (Special Performance)

First flown: 4 July 1975

The 747-SP is probably the most instantly recognisable variant of the basic 747 design. Built especially for extreme range (hence the name), the SP has about 90 percent commonality of airline-stocked parts with a conventional 747, but it has maximum take-off weight options down as low as 630,000lb

ABOVE: As soon as the E-4As were brought up to E-4B standard they developed a more purposeful appearance. Note in this picture the body-gear steering is in operation — with the inner and outer trucks pointing in different directions.

RIGHT: The SP has a significantly smaller fuselage than any other 747 model and has long been considered a favoured personal jet among Arab governments and Royal families.

BELOW RIGHT: A6-SMR is operated by the Royal Flight of Dubai. *Geoff Harber*

(285,763kg). This weight saving is derived primarily from a 48ft 5in (14.7m) shorter fuselage and a greatly simplified single-slotted flap system. The wing is the same aerodynamic shape as that on the 747-200B series but the gauge of most of the structural materials was reduced to be more in keeping with the much-lighter departure weights: this in turn allowed a considerably lighter undercarriage to be used (although it shares basically the same geometry as that used on the full-sized aircraft). To counter the reduced length of the tail-control lever arm, both structural elements were extended: the fin by 5ft (1.5m) and the stabilizer-span by 10ft (3m): the movable control surfaces are the same basic size as those on the bigger aircraft but the SP has a vertically split, double-hinged rudder to provide more bite at lower speeds.

The first SP (which eventually became N530PA for Pan American) was rolled out in a typically flamboyant Boeing paint scheme on 19 May 1975: it was flown for the first time carrying the temporary registration N747SP on 4 July that year. The radical changes to the basic 747 airframe meant that the SP had to be certified virtually as a new type and this involved nearly 550hr of validation flying by three separate aircraft, over seven months — so Pan Am had to wait until March 1976 to receive its first delivery. Overall sales of the SP were disappointing and only 45 were delivered before production ended in 1987.

747-100B

First flown: 20 June 1979

The standard -100 series airframe was modified during the late

1970s to extend the maximum take-off weight of this model up to 750,000lb (340,194kg). Non-visible structural alterations included a stronger wing/fuselage centre-section and beefed-up undercarriage. These changes allowed operators to have a much wider choice of powerplant and provided them with three different weight options: most airlines however, preferred to buy the much more attractive -200B series. The first -100B airframe (EP-IAM for Iran Air) was flown during June 1979 but only ten of this model were ever built.

747-300M Combi

First flown: 5 October 1982

The first major change to the full-sized 747 body shape was the so-called stretched upper deck (SUD) option — which was later given the designation 747-300. This aircraft was based on the -200B series fuselage, but the upper passenger deck was extended aft by 23ft 4in (7.1m): in this guise it could hold up to 91 all-economy class (six-abreast) seats, instead of the original deck's limit of 32. The circular stairs between the upper and lower cabins was replaced by a straight stairway, which allowed seven

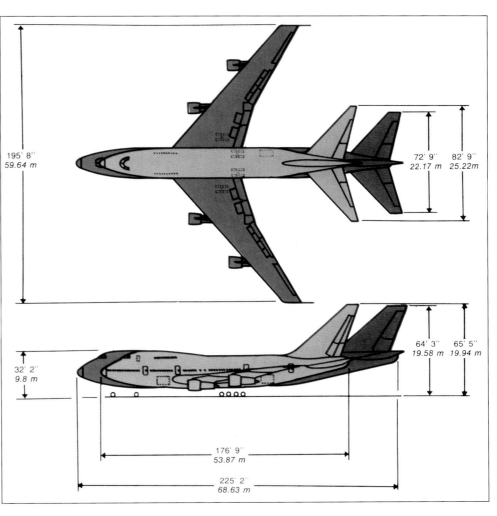

extra (economy-style) seats to be fitted on the lower deck. Evacuation regulations required that the new upper deck be fitted with two 6ft by 3½ft (1.8 x 1m) doors, in place of the

original pair of 4ft by 2ft (1.2 x 0.6m) emergency exits. The stretched upper deck was made available as a production-line option for new aircraft, or as a retrofit for existing -100 and

-200B series aircraft. The maximum take-off weight of each model remained the same as its 'ordinary' counterpart, but the operating (structure) weight was increased by 9,300lb (42,184kg) in all cases. The new forward-fuselage profile actually improved the aerodynamic efficiency of the 747, allowing its normal cruise speed to be raised from Mach 0.84 to Mach 0.85.

The first 747-300 configuration to fly (HB-IGC), was a Combi variant destined for Swissair: this aircraft flew for the first time on 5 October 1982 and the type entered service during March 1983. Boeing production records show that 12 Combis were delivered new from the Everett line, but several more have been created by the conversion of existing aircraft.

747-300

First flown: 10 December 1982

Although a Combi version was the first stretched upper deck aircraft to fly, the conventional 747-300 (without a cargo door) was by far the most popular model — with more than 60 being delivered new between early 1983 and September 1990. The basic details shown above also apply to this aircraft. In addition to the new-build aircraft shown in the production list, several -100 and -200B airframes have been converted to full -300 standard.

CORPORATE 77-43

First flown: 15 December 1983

This unlikely 747 designation follows the pattern of several Boeing jets (of various models) bought during the 1980s for personal or corporate use. In this case the designation refers to a single Pratt & Whitney-powered 747-300 (HZ-HM1A) that was specially prepared in VIP configuration for the Royal Flight of Saudi Arabia: the aircraft was first flown in December 1983 and it currently operates in a slightly modified version of Saudia's normal airline colours. The full designation is rarely (if ever) used now — with most listings preferring to show it as a 747-3G1.

747-300B

First flown: 3 December 1984

This was a strengthened and slightly heavier version of the basic all-passenger 747-300, but its sales were cut short by the success of the upgraded 747-400 series. Only five of these aircraft were built — all destined for for Korean Airlines or Singapore Airlines (the first to fly being HL7468 for Korean).

C-19A

First flown: 31 May 1985

This is the US Air Force designation covering all commercial 747s that were modified under the CRAF (Civil Reserve Air Fleet) programme. These aircraft are all -100 and -200B series passenger models that were fitted with a side cargo door and full cargo-handling system at the US taxpayers' expense. The operator gains the versatility of a virtually free Combi-style conversion, and the US Government gains by having on-demand access to the aircraft and its crew at times of national need. The first of about 20 aircraft to be converted under this programme was N655PA — a 747-121 which was re-delivered to Pan American during June 1985.

Being of Combi configuration, these aircraft can operate as passenger or cargo carriers, but the designation C-19A applies *only* when they are operating under military rules: at all other times they operate under their normal commercial designations. The last time they were called into use by the military in any numbers was during the rapid build-up towards the 1991 Gulf War.

747-300SR Short Range

First flown: 26 February 1986

This aircraft is similar in concept to the 747-100SR and owes its existence entirely to the island-hopping nature of Japanese businessmen. The structure of the standard 747-300 has been beefed-up around the wing/fuselage centre-section and undercarriage to enable the SR version to absorb many more take-off to touchdown cycles. Only six of these were ever built as new aircraft — all of them going into service with Japan Airlines.

VC-25A

First flown: 16 May 1987

The last of the Classic variants to fly, the two VC-25As are the Presidential aircraft operated by the US Government. They are basically 747-200B airframes, but differ substantially from their airliner cousins. Much of the equipment on board is still secret, but it is known that both aircraft have 747-400 style Bendix EFIS-10 (Electronic Flight Information System) cockpits; GPS and ring-laser gyro inertial navigation systems; extensive cipher, encryption and secure voice communications systems; and extra tankage to provide a range well in excess of 6,000nm (11,112km). To ensure complete self-sufficiency at any destination, the aircraft are fitted with two Garrett APU's in the tail and self-contained airstairs that emerge from the lower hold space. The cabin has appropriate office and conference facilities; a medical emergency room; rest areas for the presidential staff; and comfortable accommodation for upwards of 80 passengers.

Both airframes were assembled as 747-2G4Bs and test-flown at the Everett factory, before being handed over to Boeing's Military Airplanes Division at Wichita, Kansas, for the long conversion programme that would transform them into Presidential transports. The first completed aircraft (82-8000) was handed over to the 89th Military Airlift Wing at Andrews AFB on 23 Aug 1990, followed by the second (92-9000) on 20 December that year.

ABOVE RIGHT: Very few of the heavier weight 747-100Bs were built, with most airlines preferring to move on to the altogether more capable 200-series. Iran Air's EP-IAM was delivered during 1975. *Geoff Harber*

BELOW RIGHT: The US Air Force VC-25A is actually a much modified version of the 747-200B airframe.

6 AIRLINE OPERATORS

The following details show all the airline and air force customers for brand-new Classic 747s (used aircraft are not included but individual histories of each airframe can be traced using the listing recommended in Chapter 8). The customers are shown in chronological order of their first actual delivery. The list shows the model-numbers purchased direct from Boeing and the total number of each model delivered over the years (often as the result of a number of smaller orders). The delivery dates shown are sometimes significantly later than the first-flight date shown in the full production list: there was often a two to three-week delay for the completion of production flight-testing and fault-rectification, but any hold-up beyond that was more often than not caused by the failure of some part of the financial deal (Boeing will not release a completed aircraft until all elements of the agreed payment arrangement are firmly in place).

Each Boeing customer is allocated a two-digit designator code which will remain unchanged for many years despite changes to the airline's name — the 1950s BOAC code, for example, was 36, which was carried-over to British Airways in 1973 and remains in force today. These codes are incorporated in the factory designation of each individual Boeing airframe (across the entire product range) and are used to identify the basic specification changes that might be agreed by the customer at the time of contract signature: the code then remains with the aircraft throughout its life — no matter how many changes of ownership it may have.

BELOW: Pan American 747-121 N735PA. *Geoff Harber*

The code for each of the 747 Classic customers is shown alongside the customer names below. In most cases the listed model numbers will reflect the same customer code, but occasionally an airline will no longer want part of an order, or perhaps run into financial problems while its aircraft are actually on the production line. In such cases, the airframe is completed to the original specification (and carries the original code), but the final sale is picked up by another operator — sometimes as a means of jumping a long queue for delivery positions, or possibly because a highly attractive price is offered. As an example of this, see the two 747-227Bs delivered new to Northwest Orient Airlines, but originally ordered by Braniff.

PAN AMERICAN (21)
First delivery: 12 December 1969
The first 747 delivered to any airline was Pan Am's N733PA — a 747-121: this was one of the launch order for 25 of the type and was handed over for crew-training operations on 12 December 1969. Another eight of these aircraft were ordered direct from the factory, making 33 747-121s altogether. In addition to pioneering the basic aircraft, Pan Am also launched the 747SP programme with an order for ten, and later ordered two 747-221F cargo aircraft. All of Pan Am's 747s were powered by various marks of the Pratt & Whitney JT9D engine.

Total Classic deliveries:

747-121	33 (JT9D)
747-SP21	10 (JT9D)
747-221F	2 (JT9D)

Total Classic deliveries:
747-124   4 (JT9D)

AMERICAN AIRLINES (23)
First delivery: 18 June 1970
The first 747 operations by American Airlines were conducted with two aircraft (N740PA and N743PA) on short-term lease from Pan American: these were delivered in February and March 1970, several months in advance of the first of the airline's own production aircraft. Three batches of 747-123s were ordered in fairly quick succession — the first

OPPOSITE, ABOVE: Northwest Orient 747-151 N601US.

OPPOSITE, BELOW: Alitalia 747-243B Combi I-DEMC.

LEFT: American Airlines 747-123 N9662.

BELOW: Continental 747-124.

ABOVE: A United 747SP. *Geoff Harber*

RIGHT: Delta 747-132 N9896.

BELOW RIGHT: A retouched photo showing a Sabena 747 with a ficticious registration.

order was for ten aircraft, the second for four, and the third for just two: all 16 were configured solely as passenger aircraft and they were all delivered between 18 June 1970 and June 1971. The leased aircraft were returned to Pan Am in October 1970 and May 1971.

In common with many other carriers, American Airlines was caught out by the 1974 fuel crisis and, as passenger numbers began to fall, the requirement for very large aircraft diminished. Several of the 747-123s were sold-off at that time (one of them to NASA as the Space-Shuttle carrier) and others were converted into freighters.

Total Classic deliveries:
747-123   16 (JT9D)

UNITED AIRLINES (22)
First delivery: 30 June 1970
The first of United Airlines JT9D-powered 747-122s was delivered on 30 June 1970. Altogether three batches were ordered, totalling 18 aircraft, all of which were in service by mid-June 1973. There were no further orders for new 747s until late 1986, when a contract was signed for just two of the more-powerful 200-series aircraft: these were delivered on schedule in March 1987 as 747-222Bs. Since then all the orders for new 747s have concentrated on the upgraded 400-series.

Total Classic deliveries:
747-122   18 (JT9D)
747-222B   2 (JT9D)

NATIONAL AIRLINES (35)
First delivery: 8 September 1970
Miami-based National Airlines was a big US east-coast

domestic operator throughout the 1960s, with a substantial fleet of Boeing 727 tri-jets. Ambitious plans to develop a network of international services resulted in orders for both the 747 and the McDonnell Douglas DC-10. Only two JT9D-powered 747-135s were ordered, with deliveries scheduled for September and October 1970: internal services (from Miami to Los Angeles and New York) began in October 1970, with international routes following during the summer season of 1972. Before any of the long-range sectors could really become established, National began to suffer badly from falling yields in the wake of the 1973/74 fuel crisis: both 747s were withdrawn from use in August 1975 and sold (to Northwest Airlines) about a year later.

Total Classic deliveries:
747-135   2 (JT9D)

DELTA AIRLINES (32)
First delivery: 2 October 1970
Although Delta is among the biggest airlines in the world, it has never had much of a requirement for the 747: five of the early Pratt & Whitney-powered 100-series aircraft were delivered between 2 October 1970 and 11 November 1971, but the

other variants have never been ordered. Of those that *were* delivered, two were quickly disposed of when the price of jet fuel shot-up during the early 1970s and the other three were sold during the spring of 1977.

Total Classic deliveries:
747-132   5 (JT9D)

IBERIA (56)
First delivery: 2 October 1970
The Spanish flag-carrier Iberia originally ordered two 747-156 aircraft for delivery in October and November 1970: these replaced DC-8s on the Madrid–New York route before the end of the year and then went on to link Madrid and Barcelona with major cities in Canada and the Spanish-speaking areas of South America: these longer-range services were not well-suited to the 100-series aircraft, so a single 747-256B was ordered for delivery in January 1972. These three aircraft soldiered-on until early 1980, when the first of a new batch of six -256Bs arrived: at this point Iberia standardised on the 200-series and the two original -156s were sold to TWA. Current plans suggest that the 200-series will remain in service until about 2003.

Total Classic deliveries:
747-156   2 (JT9D)
747-256B   7 (JT9D)

SABENA (29)
First delivery: 19 November 1970
The first of two 747-129s was delivered to the Belgian flag carrier Sabena on 19 November 70, followed by the second on 4 December: at that time they were both configured as standard passenger models. After a short period of crew training and route-proving the aircraft were introduced into service between Brussels–New York in February 1971. The rise in fuel prices during the early 1970s had such a severe effect on passenger revenues, that Sabena was on the verge of selling the 747s and reverting to the much smaller Boeing 707. To prevent the need for this — not just for Sabena, but for other carriers

who were clearly thinking along the same lines — Boeing engineers devised a side cargo door for the rear fuselage of the 747. This development enabled cargo capacity to be vastly increased on lean passenger-routes and the extra revenue certainly saved the day for Sabena. The two aircraft were returned to Boeing for conversion at the beginning of 1974: the transformation reduced the available passenger capacity from 365 to 242 and resulted in the designation being changed to 747-129 (SCD). More importantly perhaps, the cargo door conversion was adopted by many other airlines and the idea was offered as an option on the production line: any new aircraft fitted with a side cargo door was given the model designation 747 Combi.

The two JT9D-powered 747-129s remained in service for about 20 years, but in June 1986 the first 747-329 arrived in Brussels, followed by a second in September 1990. Both of these aircraft had been fitted with cargo doors on the production line and were correctly called Combi models: Sabena had also switched to General Electric CF6 powerplants.

Total Classic deliveries:
747-129   2 (JT9D)
747-329 Combi   2 (CF6)

AER LINGUS (48)
First delivery: 15 December 1970
Aer Lingus was another of those national flag-carrier airlines that simply had to have 747s in the early 1970s in order to remain competitive on a small number of vital routes: whether or not such carriers were right, or whether they ever made money out of the aircraft, must be open to question. In the case of the Irish state-owned airline, two JT9D-powered 100-series aircraft were delivered on 15 December 1970 and 18 March 1971 — basically to replace Boeing 707s on services between Dublin and the USA. Even one aircraft generated an enormous increase in seating capacity on these routes, but the second was considered essential to guarantee the service against technical problems. In the event, traffic suffered badly after the OPEC oil crisis and two aircraft could no longer be

justified: thereafter one or other of them was often out on medium/long-term lease (so much so, that Aer Lingus occasionally had to resort to leasing an aircraft *in* to handle a busy summer season).

Total Classic deliveries:
747-148   2 (JT9D)

BRANIFF INTERNATIONAL (27)
First delivery: 5 January 1971
Braniff originally ordered two 747-127s to operate its daily commuter-type services between Dallas/Fort Worth and Honolulu, but only one of these was ever delivered (N601BN, which was handed over on 5 January 1971). Boeing agreed to cancel the second aircraft in return for an increased order for 727-200s, and the 747 delivery position was later sold — still carrying the Braniff customer code — to Wardair of Canada. There were no further 747 orders from Braniff until the airline decided to go fully international during the late 1970s. New

a lower-deck kitchen (which occupied part of the under-floor baggage compartment), before being loaded into an elevator and dispatched to a 'service-centre' in the cabin above.

After operating for more than seven years with Pratt & Whitney as its exclusive powerplant supplier, Qantas suddenly switched its allegiance to Rolls-Royce and all new aircraft delivered after the end of 1978 were equipped with RB.211s — the first of these being VH-ECB, a 747-238B Combi which arrived in Sydney during November 1979. Over the following two years three conventional 747-238Bs; another -238B Combi and two RB.211-powered 747-SP38s were delivered. The final Classics ordered by Qantas were six 747-338s, all of which had entered service before the end of May 1987.

Contrary to general trends within the industry, Qantas was reported at the end of 1998 to be looking for up to six additional RB.211-powered Classics and is paying particular attention to the disposal plans of BA and Cathay Pacific.

Total Classic deliveries:

747-238B	16 (JT9D)
747-238B Combi	1 (JT9D)
747-238B Combi	2 (RB.211)
747-238B	3 (RB.211)
747-SP38	2 (RB.211)
747-338	6 (RB.211)

SOUTH AFRICAN AIRWAYS (44)

First delivery: 22 October 1971

The arrival in Johannesburg of the first of SAA's 747s signalled the entry into service of yet another small change to the basic aircraft design. All earlier 747s had been fitted with auxiliary blow-in doors around the intake lips in order to improve the inlet capacity (and therefore mass-flow through the engine) during take-off. Airframe No.154 (ZS-SAL) was the first 747 to incorporate additional sound-deadening material around the nacelles, which required larger diameter intakes and the deletion of all blow-in doors: these 'solid' intakes eventually became standard on all production aircraft and the modification was retrospectively applied to most existing airframes. ZS-SAL was also the first production

example to be fitted with the more powerful 7-series JT9D engines and it was retained by Boeing for some time to conduct the certification trials. As a result, the first 747 actually delivered to SAA was ZS-SAN on 22 October 1971: this aircraft was used for crew training and route-proving trials until its sister-ship (ZS-SAM) arrived in December 1971, at which time the 747 was first put into service on the Johannesburg–London route. All five 747-244Bs (including ZS-SAL) were delivered before the end of '72 and international routes previously operated by Boeing 707s were gradually taken over.

During February 1976 the first of six 747-SP44s was introduced on longer-range sectors — such as the popular non-stop route between Capetown–London. Two 747-244B Combis (one of which would later crash into the Indian Ocean after a fire in the cargo compartment) were delivered during 1980, and the last of SAA's Classics — two stretched upper-deck 747-344s — were introduced into service during the spring of 1983.

Late 1998, SAA was reported to be negotiating leases for an additional 200-series freighter and 'several more' 747-300s: talks are thought to be in progress with both Swissair and SIA.

Total Classic deliveries:

747-244B	5 (JT9D)
747-SP44	6 (JT9D)
747-244B Combi	2 (JT9D)
747-344	2 (JT9D)

ABOVE RIGHT: Korean 747-SPB5 HL7456.

BELOW: World Airways 747-200C.

TAP — Air Portugal (82)

First delivery: 16 February 1972

Anticipating an increasing level of traffic between Lisbon and some of its colonial past in Africa and South America, TAP (*Transportes Aereos Portugueses*) ordered two 747-282Bs in 1971 and additional examples in early 1974 and the summer of 1985. All four aircraft were delivered on schedule (CS-TJA arriving first on 16 February 1972) but the major oil crisis of 1973/74 intervened and airline profitability suffered all over the world. TAP services began with Lisbon–New York in March 1972, but 747 routes to the old colonies were delayed — initially by the lack of passengers, and then by political problems in Africa. The first two aircraft remained in service for about twelve years before they were finally sold to TWA, but the second pair were desperately under-utilised by TAP and remained at Lisbon for only about a year before being sold to Pakistan International Airlines.

Total Classic deliveries:

747-282B	4 (JT9D)

WARDAIR — CANADA (11)

First delivery: 23 April 1973

Wardair began 747 operations with a JT9D-powered 100-series aircraft that had been manufactured to Braniff specifications but never delivered that airline. The airframe was built and test-flown in March 1971 as a 747-127, but before its final completion Braniff had agreed with Boeing to trade-in its value against a number of new 727-200s: the aircraft was then stored for nearly two years, before being converted to a hybrid 747-1D1 specification and sold to Wardair for delivery in April 1973 (a second airframe was converted to the same specification and sold to Wardair in 1974, but this was an ex-Continental aircraft that had already been in service for three years). As a charter company, Wardair specialised in trans-Atlantic operations from all the major cities in Canada to various centres in Europe: 747 services began in May 1973 on routes between Canada and the United Kingdom.

After nearly five years of operations with the two 100-series aircraft, Wardair enlarged its fleet by the acquisition of two brand-new 747-211Bs for 1978 and 1979 delivery. These were built to the company's own specification and differed from the first pair, mainly because they were powered by GE CF6-50 engines. Wardair itself lost its separate identity in October 1989, when it was merged into the Canadian Airlines International group.

Total Classic deliveries:

747-127/1D1	1 (JT9D)
747-211B	2 (CF6)

WORLD AIRWAYS (73)

First delivery: 27 April 1973

The US charter carrier World Airways was the first to order and operate the Convertible (-200C) model of the 747, which incorporated a nose cargo door *and* a full set of passenger windows on the upper and main decks. The first two 747-273Cs were delivered in April and May 1973, and a third arrived during June 1974. Although this third aircraft was owned by World Airways, it was never operated by them — instead, it spent virtually a decade employed on long leases to a variety of other carriers. The first two *did* appear in World Airways colours: they operated trans-Atlantic passenger services all through the summer of 1973, and then capitalised on their freight-handling capability by operating full-time cargo charters for the US military during the following winter. After one more season of passenger operation (summer 1974), both the original aircraft were withdrawn from service by World Airways and spent most of their remaining time with the airline leased out to other carriers. The first two were sold in November 1983 and the third had gone by May 1987.

Total Classic deliveries:

747-273C   3 (JT9D)

KOREAN AIRLINES (B5)

First delivery: 1 May 1973

Between May 1973 and end 1988 Korean Airlines purchased 16 Classics — all powered by P&W JT9Ds and representing several different model types. The early aircraft were fitted with a main-deck baggage-handling system — an option that allowed passenger baggage to be loaded into small containers and carried in the rear of the main cabin (known as Zone-E): this released the two big underfloor compartments for containers, but it reduced the seating capacity to about 320. The first two 747-2B5Bs were delivered during spring/summer 1973 and went into service on a new route that took them to Los Angeles, via Tokyo and Honolulu. Two additional -2B5Bs were delivered in spring 1979, followed by the first of a large order for assorted 747 models. This rapid expansion involved three 747-2B5F cargo aircraft, two 747-SPB5s, two more conventional -2B5Bs and two stretched-upper-deck 747-3B5s — all delivered between June 1980 and March 1985. The final Classic order concentrated heavily on cargo operations — with one 747-3B5 Combi and two more -2B5F freighters, all delivered autumn 1988.

Total Classic deliveries:

747-2B5B	6 (JT9D)
747-2B5F	5 (JT9D)
747-SPB5	2 (JT9D)
747-3B5	2 (JT9D)
747-3B5 Combi	1 (JT9D)

OLYMPIC AIRWAYS (84)

First delivery: 21 June 1973

The two JT9D-powered 747-284Bs ordered by Olympic Airways were delivered to Athens during June and December 1973. Services began on the Athens to New York run in July 1973 and were later expanded to include regular flights to Sydney and Singapore. The first aircraft (SX-OAA) was sold to Trans World Airlines during 1985, but the second (SX-OAB) remains with Olympic and operates alongside three used 747-212Bs acquired during 1984/85 from Singapore Airlines. Five A340s have recently been acquired and most of them should be delivered before the end of 2000: at that time the 747s will be retired.

Total Classic deliveries:

747-284B	2 (JT9D)

US AIR FORCE (G4)

First delivery: 16 July 1973

During February 1973 the Electronic Systems Division of the US Air Force ordered two JT9D-powered 747-200B airframes as Phase One of the *481B Advanced Airborne Command Post (AABNCP)* programme: a third airframe was ordered in July 1973 and a fourth in December of the same year — these later orders differed from the first pair because they were to be powered by General Electric F103-GE-100 engines (the military equivalent of a CF6 turbofan). All four airframes were to be delivered in a basic 'green' condition, before undergoing an extensive refit and modification programme to transform them into three E-4A and one E-4B command-post aircraft. The three E-4As (two JT9D and one F103-powered) were all fitted with existing mission-equipment packages transferred from a trio of EC-135J command-post aircraft (based on the Boeing 707 airframe): this would give the E-4As a basic *National Emergency Airborne Command Post (NEACP)* capability. The first aircraft was delivered in this condition to Andrews AFB in December 1974. Lessons learned during the transfer and integration of the electronics, plus a year or two of operational experience as E-4As, laid the foundations for a major upgrade of the whole system. The fourth airframe was fitted with a completely new battlefield electronics suite, a new electrical system, an in-flight fuel receiving system and many other changes that brought it up to full E-4B (AABNCP) standard. The first fully-equipped E-4B (75-0125) was delivered to the US Air Force for operational service on 21 December 1979: during June 1980 the first contract was signed to bring all three E-4As up to full E-4B standard — which included changing the engines of both JT9D-powered examples to the General Electric F103-GE-100. The updates were completed individually and the aircraft were returned to operational service in 1983, 1984 and 1985.

Two additional aircraft were ordered by the US Government during 1986: these were the basic 747-2G4B airframes which later became VC-25A military transports — better known perhaps as the Presidential aircraft, *Air Force One*. These were also equipped with General Electric military engines (achieving a common standard with the E-4Bs) and were designed to replace the two VC-137Cs — Boeing 707-320s — that had become so familiar in the Presidential role. Both 747 airframes were initially flown during 1987, but an extensive refit (see main text) delayed their entry into service until the latter half of 1990.

Total Classic deliveries:

E-4A	2 (JT9D)
E-4A	1 (F103)
E-4B	1 (F103)
VC-25A	2 (F103)

SINGAPORE AIRLINES (12)

First delivery: 31 July 1973

During October 1972 Malaysia-Singapore Airlines (MSA) ceased operations as a single entity and split into two separate carriers — Malaysian Airline System (MAS — subsequently renamed Malaysia Airlines) and Singapore International Airlines (SIA — later shortened to Singapore Airlines). Both started life with second-hand 707s, but SIA quickly added four new 707s and then ordered its first batch of four 747-212Bs (two firm and two on option): the first two of these aircraft (9V-SIA and 9V-SIB) were delivered during July and August 1973, but the confirmed options did not arrive until July 1974 and February 1975. Since then, the airline has become one of the biggest and most successful operators of the 747, having bought and disposed of a total fleet of 34 new Classics, before moving on to its present (2000) fleet of nearly 50 400-series. The only Classics still owned by SIA are a few remaining 300-series — and they are all leased to other operators, or in storage awaiting a buyer.

Total Classic deliveries:

747-212B	19 (JT9D)
747-312	11 (JT9D)
747-212F	1 (JT9D)
747-312 Combi	3 (JT9D)

CP AIR (17)

First delivery: 15 November 1973

Vancouver-based CP Air (formerly known as Canadian Pacific Airways) ordered four JT9D-powered 747-217Bs in 1973 — the first pair for delivery in November and December of that year and the second pair timed to arrive exactly a year later.

Because of its geographical position on the western coast of Canada, most of CP's business was centred on trans-Pacific routes to Far East destinations and over-the-pole routes to Europe: the 747s were introduced on the Tokyo–Hong Kong sectors during December 1973, followed by scheduled flights to Amsterdam, Rome and London during 1974. The four aircraft were delivered in a striking new red and orange paint scheme, with much bare metal on the lower fuselage: they were destined to replace a fleet of Douglas DC-8s. The airline itself — which had been formed in 1942 by the old Canadian Pacific Railways Company — was merged with several other carriers in March 1987 to form the Canadian Airlines International group (which itself has just been absorbed into Air Canada).

Total Classic deliveries:

747-217B	4 (JT9D)

ABOVE: CP Air's 747-217B C-FCRA was sold to Pakistan Airlines in 1986.

BELOW: Singapore Airlines 747-212B 9V-SIA.

BELOW LEFT: The first E-4A airframe (73-1676) was later converted to this F103-GE-100-powered E-4B configuration.

SEABOARD WORLD AIRLINES (45)

First delivery: 31 July 1974

One of the two major US cargo carriers of the 1960s and 1970s, Seaboard World placed the first big order for the 747-200F. Only one of this specialised model had previously been ordered (for Lufthansa in late 1971) and Seaboard's order for up to six 747-245Fs must have come as a big relief to Boeing, which had invested a lot of money in the design and certification of the aircraft. The new order differed from the original Lufthansa 747-230F in that all the -245Fs had a side cargo door installed — making it a much more flexible aircraft, capable of handling bigger freight containers. Although Seaboard specialised in trans-Atlantic *cargo* flights, its 747s were all delivered with full passenger amenities (including windows) on the upper deck: this enabled the airline to carry up to 16 service personnel while the aircraft were engaged on military charter flights. Of the six aircraft ordered, only four were delivered before Seaboard merged with the other big US cargo airline, Flying Tiger Line (see details later).

MIDDLE EAST AIRLINES (B4)

First delivery: 20 May 1975

The three 747-2B4B Combis ordered by MEA were consecutive aircraft on the production line and all were delivered between May and August 1975: thereafter, however, they did not have a happy time. Arriving at Beirut Airport at the beginning of a virtual civil war, they were conspicuous objects and often became targets for small-arms and rocket-grenade fire. The aircraft did enter scheduled service on routes to London and Paris, but the timetable was always a hit-and-miss affair due to fighting around Beirut airport and much of their time was spent parked in the relative safety of Larnaca Airport on Cyprus.

By mid-1977 it was realised that the passenger loads available to MEA could no longer support such a big aircraft and they were withdrawn from use to begin a long series of leasing arrangements. The 747s were occasionally flown by MEA between leases, but the operation was never truly successful.

Total Classic deliveries:

747-245F(SCD)　　　　4 (JT9D)

Total Classic deliveries:

747-2B4B Combi　　　　3 (JT9D)

LEFT: BAe 146 wing being loaded onto a Seaboard World 747-245F.

RIGHT: IranAir's 747-286B Combis are regular visitors to Heathrow. *Hugh Newell*

BELOW: MEA 747-2B4B Combi N203AE. *Hugh Newell*

IRAN AIR (86)

First delivery: 12 March 1976

Another politically troubled airline, Iran Air was making spectacular progress until the Shah was toppled and US Embassy staff were taken hostage in 1979: at that time both the airline and the Iranian Air Force were subjected to US economic sanctions, which had a significant effect on both new aircraft orders and the provision of spares and support for those already in service. The airline began 747 operations in 1976 when two JT9D-powered 747-SP86s were introduced on the Tehran–London–New York service. These were quickly followed by two 747-286B Combis, and then by another pair of SPs: the route map had also been expanded to include regular services to Paris, Rome, Frankfurt and Kuwait. Boeing had also received an order for four 747-186Bs when the political problems got in the way: one was delivered more or less on time, but the other three had to be cancelled.

Total Classic deliveries:

747-SP86	4 (JT9D)
747-286B Combi	2 (JT9D)
747-186B	1 (JT9D)

SYRIANAIR (94)

First delivery: 21 May 1976

The Syrian flag-carrying airline (formally Syrian Arab Airlines, but better known by its operating title Syrianair) has only ever operated two 747 aircraft: these were the two 747-SP94s that were delivered in 1976 and remain in service today. The choice of the ultra long-range SP seems slightly odd because the route

network has never included long trans-oceanic flights. Services began in June 1976 on the Damascus–London sector and were subsequently expanded to include other cities in Europe, the Gulf region and the Far East.

Total Classic deliveries:
747-SP94   2 (JT9D)

IRAQI AIRWAYS (70)
First delivery: 24 June 1976
Iraqi Airways began 747 operations with a pair of JT9D-powered 747-270C (Convertibles) in the summer of 1976: a third aircraft was added to the fleet in July 1982. During the early 1980s the Iraqi Government purchased a single 747-SP70 for VIP duties: this aircraft was 'mothered' by the state airline and generally flown by senior airline crew — but it was not part of the Iraqi Airways fleet. The Iraqi -270Cs were the first Convertible 747s to be fitted with a Combi-style side cargo door and the Boeing-designed on-board cargo loader. All domestic and international air services by Iraqi carriers have effectively been banned by the UN since the end of the Gulf War: the fate of all four aircraft is unclear, although at least two of them are thought to have survived the hostilities.

Total Classic deliveries:
747-270C   3 (JT9D)
747-SP70 (VIP) 1 (JT9D)

ABOVE: Cargolux 747 Convertible N537MC. *Richard Potts*

ABOVE LEFT: UTA 747-2B3B Combi F-BTDG. *Hugh Newell*

BELOW LEFT: ANA 747-281B Combi JA8181.

limited by government decree to a small number of charter flights to destinations such as Beijing, Hong Kong, Manila and Singapore. A conventional 747 was not really suited to this kind of route network and ANA resisted buying the aircraft until the specialised 747SR was developed (see main text). The high-capacity SR (short-range) option could replace multiple 727 or TriStar flights to a single destination and as soon as ANA received government permission to do so, it began to order the aircraft: between December 1978 and November 1982 no fewer than 17 747-SR81s were delivered — all the result of small order batches accounting for an average of four aircraft each time. Unlike JAL, all the ANA 747s were powered by General Electric CF6 engines. In 1985 ANA was encouraged to compete with JAL on some of the longer-range international routes — particularly those to Europe and the United States. It then ordered four conventional 747-281Bs for delivery during 1986 and 1987. Most of the international flights are now operated by 747-400s, but the earlier aircraft are still occasional visitors to UK.

Total Classic deliveries:

747-SR81	17 (CF6)
747-281B	4 (CF6)

AIR MADAGASCAR (B2)
First delivery: 26 January 1979
A single JT9D-powered 747-2B2B Combi (5R-MFT) was delivered to Air Madagascar at the beginning of 1979 and has

been in service ever since — connecting the capital Antananarivo with Paris, using the alternating stopover points of Nairobi and Marseille; Djibouti and Jeddah; or Djibouti and Rome.

Total Classic deliveries:

747-2B2B Combi	1 (JT9D)

CARGOLUX (R7)
First delivery: 31 January 1979
One of the longest-lasting and most successful all-cargo airlines, Cargolux added a single 747-2R7F to its existing fleet of DC-8 and CL-44 freighters in January 1979: a second was delivered in October 1980. Both aircraft were fitted with the optional side cargo door and windows in the upper deck compartment. The 747s were initially used on a semi-scheduled out-and-return run between Luxembourg–Hong Kong, with an eastbound stopover in the Gulf and return stops alternating between Taipei and Vienna. Most of the long-range sectors are now flown by 747-400s but the two original aircraft remain in service.

Total Classic deliveries:

747-2R7F	2 (JT9D)

AVIANCA (59)
First delivery: 8 June 1979
Between 1976 and 1995 Avianca operated a number of different 100 and 200-series 747s — most of them on long or short-term leases from other carriers. The only new aircraft actually owned by the airline was a 747-259B Combi (HK-2300), which arrived in Bogota in June 1979. Even this machine proved to be a huge financial burden to the Colombian economy, so in 1983

ABOVE: PIA's CF6-powered 747-240B Combi (AP-BAK).

ABOVE RIGHT: Flying Tigers 747-249F N807FT. *Alan Bushell*

BELOW RIGHT: Philippine Airlines 747-2F6B N742PR.

it was sold to a US brokerage company and immediately leased back (as HK-2980X): in this form it remained in service with Avianca until it was replaced at the beginning of 1995 by Extended Range (ER) versions of the Boeing 767.

Total Classic deliveries:

747-259B Combi   1 (JT9D)

SAUDI ARABIAN GOVERNMENT (68 + G1)

First delivery: 11 July 1979

The first 747 to be operated as a so-called Biz-jet, was the 747-SP68 purchased by the Saudi Arabian Government for the personal use of King Khaled and his entourage: the contract was signed at the end of 1977, the airframe flew for the first time in its 'green' form on 28 August 1978 and was finally fitted-out and delivered (as HZ-HM1) on 11 July 1979. Little is known about the operation of this aircraft, but reports at the time suggested that it was largely equipped as a mobile hospital — ready to rush the king to America in the event of his continuing ill health. The aircraft was the first SP to be powered by Rolls-Royce RB.211 engines: it was given the Boeing customer-code number (68) of Saudia Airlines and flown in a slightly modified Saudia colour scheme. The only visible difference between this and the national airline SPs was the extensive range of communications antennas along the dorsal spine of the aircraft. At the end of 1983 the Government added a 747-3G1 (HZ-HM1A) to the VIP fleet. Although it was delivered in the same Saudia colours as the SP, this machine had a totally different customer code number (G1) and was unique among the Saudi-owned aircraft because it was powered by Pratt & Whitney JT9D-7R4G2 engines (all the others are Rolls-Royce powered). Both VIP aircraft were still in service at the time of writing.

Total Classic deliveries:

747-SP68	1 (RB.211)
747-3G1	1 (JT9D)

CATHAY PACIFIC AIRWAYS (67)

First delivery: 20 July 1979

Hong Kong-based Cathay Pacific has always been one of the most enthusiastic operators of Rolls-Royce-powered 747s: all its aircraft — including the current crop of 400-series — have been powered this way. The first four 747-267Bs were ordered for delivery in 1979 and 1980 and the first aircraft (VR-HKG) arrived on schedule during July 1979 — quickly replacing the Boeing 707 on a route from Hong Kong–Melbourne and Sydney. By the end of May 1984 a total of eight 200-series had been delivered and the route network expanded to include major commercial centres in all five continents. During June 1985 the first of six higher-capacity 747-367s was delivered, followed in September 1987 by the first (of two) 747-267F dedicated freighters. The last Classic delivery to the airline — the second freighter — was made in March 1990: all subsequent orders focused on the digital 400-series aircraft.

Cathay retired the bulk of its 200-series during 1998, and in March 1999 it was announced that all six -300s had been leased to PIA for two years, with an additional 10-year option after that.

Total Classic deliveries:

747-267B	8 (RB.211)
747-367	6 (RB.211)
747-267F	2 (RB.211)

PAKISTAN INTERNATIONAL AIRLINES (40)

First delivery: 26 July 1979

Although PIA has operated up to eight 200-series 747s, only two of them have been bought new from the factory — all the others have either been purchased on the used-aircraft market, or lease-purchased from an earlier operator. The airline began its 747 operations with two JT9D-powered 747-282Bs, which were leased from the Portuguese carrier TAP in April 1976 and finally purchased in April 1980. During the currency of the lease arrangement, PIA decided to buy its own aircraft and ordered two 747-240B Combis direct from Boeing: curiously, these two were powered by CF6 engines. The outright purchase of the ex-TAP aircraft was then confirmed, and both engine types operated in parallel until four 747-217Bs were acquired from CP Air: these were all delivered to Pakistan between December 1985 and November 1986. The choice of the Canadian aircraft, all powered by JT9D engines , appeared to reverse PIA's earlier decision to select CF6 engines for its own aircraft. All eight of these 747s remained in service until end 1998, but PIA has now announced that it intends to retire all six JT9D-powered aircraft and replace them with six ex-Cathay Pacific 300-series — which are all powered by Rolls-Royce engines!

Total Classic deliveries:

747-240B Combi	2 (CF6)

FLYING TIGER LINE (49)

First delivery: 31 October 1979

Where Seaboard World Airlines (see above) specialised in trans-Atlantic operations, Flying Tiger Line concentrated almost entirely on trans-Pacific routes. Both were major US cargo airlines and both placed big orders for the JT9D-powered 747-200F. Flying Tiger began 747 operations with a number of ex-passenger 100-series aircraft, which were converted into freighters with the addition of a side cargo door: the first arrived in August 1974 and the sixth (and last) was delivered in May 1977. These aircraft gradually took over from DC-8Fs and soon became a familiar sight on westbound routes such as Chicago–Anchorage–Tokyo–Taipei. Four new 747-249Fs were ordered during 1978: these were true cargo aircraft in every sense of the word, with strengthened floor, roller-conveyer cargo handling equipment and both nose and side-opening cargo doors. These were delivered between October 1979 and August 1980. Flying Tiger had been buying large quantities of Seaboard World shares since 1977 and in 1980 the two companies merged under the Flying Tiger name — thus creating the largest all-cargo airline in the world. With this merger, Flying Tiger 'inherited' not only Seaboard's existing fleet, but also its outstanding orders, including two 747-245Fs which were both delivered new to the expanded airline in October 1980 and are shown below, rather than in the Seaboard World section.

Total Classic deliveries:

747-249F	4 (JT9D)
747-245F	2 (JT9D)

THAI AIRWAYS INTERNATIONAL (D7)

First delivery: 2 November 1979

The 1980s was a decade of great expansion for Thai Airways International. It added the 747 to an already successful fleet of Douglas DC-8s, DC-10s and Airbus A300B4s, and opened up a number of new routes to Europe and the United States. The first 747s were a batch of three CF6-powered 747-2D7Bs ordered in 1979: these were all delivered by February 1980. One additional aircraft was ordered early in 1980, and two more were added for 1981 and 1984 delivery. The fleet remained unchanged until 1987, when the first of two 300-series aircraft arrived: thereafter all orders concentrated on the two-crew 400-series. By the end of 1998 the pair of -3D7s were still in service, but most of the original 200-series had been retired.

Total Classic deliveries:

747-2D7B	6 (CF6)
747-3D7	2 (CF6)

PHILIPPINE AIRLINES (F6)

First delivery: 21 December 1979

Philippine Airlines ordered four CF6-powered 747-2F6Bs during 1979 and these were all delivered (carrying consecutive US registrations) by the end of 1980. They were originally introduced on the route from Manila–San Francisco via Honolulu, but the network was rapidly expanded to include Amsterdam, Bangkok, Frankfurt and Rome: these routes had previously been flown by various models of the Douglas DC-8. Although no additional 747s were ordered direct from the factory, several used 200-series passenger-aircraft and Combis (powered by both Pratt & Whitney and General Electric engines) were acquired during the 1980s and 1990s. All the Classics were retired some time ago and the 747 fleet now consists entirely of the two-crew 400-series. At the time of writing, Philippine Airlines has ceased operations due to financial problems.

Total Classic deliveries:

747-2F6B   4 (CF6)

TRANSAMERICA (71)

First delivery: 21 December 1979

US supplemental carrier Trans International Airlines merged with Saturn Airways in December 1976 and briefly became the largest cargo charter airline in the world, under the new name Transamerica. Five CF6-powered 747-271Cs were ordered during 1979 but only three were delivered before the airline ran into trouble and ceased trading in the 1980s: the two outstanding orders were cancelled and the airframes were never built. Some operations were flown with the aircraft that had been delivered, but a large part of their time was spent leased out to other carriers. All three were sold during 1987 — two to International Lease Finance Corporation, and one to Cargolux.

Total Classic deliveries:

747-271C   3 (CF6)

CAAC — AIR CHINA (J6)

First delivery: 29 February 1980

The Civil Aviation Administration of China (CAAC) emerged

from a long period of self-imposed isolationism during the 1960s and began to order western airliners — starting with British Viscounts in 1963 and then Tridents in 1972: a big ideological barrier was overcome early in 1973, with the arrival of the first of ten Boeing 707s. The acquisition of this improved equipment encouraged CAAC to expand from a broadly domestic route network into the international arena. The first 747 operations were conducted during 1978 with a small number of SPs on individual short-term leases from Pan Am: these were used for a series of round-trip charters between Shanghai and San Francisco. The flights were so successful that CAAC bought its own aircraft in 1979 — three to its own 747-SPJ6 specification and one 747-SP27, which had been built to a Braniff specification and stored (undelivered) for more than two years. All four aircraft were powered by JT9D engines, and all four were delivered between January and December 1980. As the route-map expanded, CAAC needed more passenger capacity and less range: a single 200-series aircraft was ordered early in 1983, followed by two more in 1985 and 1987. The final Classic ordered by Air China (a new name for the airline, granted in 1988) was a single 747-2J6F which arrived during October 1990. All subsequent orders from Air China were for the upgraded 400-series.

Total Classic deliveries:

747-SPJ6	3 (JT9D)
747-SP27	1 (JT9D)
747-2J6B	3 (JT9D)
747-2J6F	1 (JT9D)

ABOVE RIGHT: **Varig 747-2L5B Combi PP-VNA.**

BELOW: **Air China's B-2448 is a 747-2J6B Combi, delivered December 1985.** *Hugh Newell*

BELOW RIGHT: **Cameroon Airlines 747-2H7B Combi TJ-CAB.**

GARUDA (U3)

First delivery: 2 July 1980

The Indonesian flag-carrier Garuda purchased four JT9D-powered 747-2U3Bs at the end of 1979 and they were all delivered and in service by the end of August 1980: two additional aircraft were ordered in 1981 and delivered early in 1982. Reflecting the Dutch-colonial background of Indonesia the first 747 services were flown to Amsterdam, but the aircraft was soon connecting Jakarta with many other cities in Europe, Asia and Australia — largely replacing older DC-8s on the routes, but in some cases replacing the DC-10. During the early 1990s Garuda acquired three 400-series aircraft (two new 747-4U3s and an ex-Varig 747-441) but at the time of writing at least three of the Classics are still in service and are regular winter season visitors to Gatwick.

Total Classic deliveries:

747-2U3B	6 (JT9D)

AIR AFRIQUE (S4)

First delivery: 3 October 1980

The multinational flag-carrier Air Afrique has had a rolling membership of about ten partners — all of them small (in terms of financial resources) nations which share a common heritage of being former French colonies: the airline was set up in 1961 and was initially 'mothered' by Air France. Jet equipment has included Caravelles, DC-8s and DC-10s, and in 1980 a single JT9D-powered 747-2S4F was ordered — primarily to carry industrial components from France into Africa and agricultural products on the return journey. Registered in the Ivory Coast as TU-TAP, the aircraft was delivered during October 1980 but was only retained for about three years. Early in 1984 it was leased out to Saudia for 12 months and then to Cargolux, before being sold to a leasing company.

Total Classic deliveries:

747-2S4F	1 (JT9D)

VARIG (41)

First delivery: 30 January 1981

The Brazilian carrier Varig began its 747 operations with three CF6-powered 747-2L5B Combi aircraft, which were built to a Libyan Arab Airlines specification but not delivered because of political problems. Varig agreed to take them — presumably at a very favourable price — and they were all taken out of storage for delivery to Rio de Janeiro during the first three months of 1981. The aircraft were used very successfully for several years, primarily replacing 707s on some of the

longer-range routes. When more passenger-capacity was needed, Varig turned to the stretched upper-deck 300-series and ordered two 747-341 Combis to operate alongside its existing fleet: this time the airframes were prepared to Varig's own technical specification, but the CF6 engines were retained. The new Combis were delivered in December 1985, and the fleet was completed during the spring of 1988 with the arrival of three passenger-only 747-341s.

Total Classic deliveries:

747-2L5B Combi	3	(CF6)
747-341 Combi	2	(CF6)
747-341	3	(CF6)

CAMEROON AIRLINES (H7)
First delivery: 26 February 1981
One of the founding members of the Air Afrique consortium, the Cameroun government decided to break away from the group in 1971 and form its own national carrier — which later became Cameroon Airlines. Long range routes to Europe were initially flown with a 707-3H7C but in 1980 a single JT9D-powered 747 was ordered in the form of a 747-2H7B Combi. This aircraft was delivered to Douala in February 1981 and remains in service today.

Total Classic deliveries:

747-2H7B Combi	1	(JT9D)

SAUDIA (68)
First delivery: 2 April 1981
Saudia began its wide-body operations in the late 1970s with RB.211-powered Lockheed TriStars — which had basically been designed for US domestic routes and lacked the range for trans-Atlantic services: at that time all the airline's oceanic routes were being flown by Boeing 707s. The first 747s were three JT9D-powered 200-series Combis which were leased

from MEA: these arrived during 1977/78 and were followed in 1979 by a single all-passenger aircraft leased from Korean Airlines. A fleet of new 747s was ordered in 1980: to ensure engine commonality with the earlier TriStars, these aircraft were delivered with Rolls-Royce engines. The first order consisted of five 747-168Bs (a heavier version of the basic 100-series aircraft) and a single 747-SP68: these were all delivered during the first six months of 1981. A second batch of identical aircraft (three more -168Bs and an additional SP68) arrived before the end of April 1982. The fleet then remained the same (apart from the return of all four leased aircraft) until a batch of 10 747-368s was delivered between June 1985 and August 1986. A single 747-268F cargo aircraft was delivered during December 1988.

Total Classic deliveries:

747-168B	8 (RB.211)
747-SP68	2 (RB.211)
747-368	10 (RB.211)
747-268F	1 (RB.211)

AIR NEW ZEALAND (19)
First delivery: 22 May 1981

To replace DC-8s and DC-10s on its extensive trans-Pacific route network, Air New Zealand ordered four RB.211-powered 747-219Bs at the beginning of 1981. The first three of these virtually followed each other down the Everett assembly line and arrived in Auckland between February and June 1981. There was then a gap of nearly a year (during which a fifth aircraft was added to the overall order) and the final two were delivered in June and August 1982. All five are still in service, together with eight 747-400s.

Total Classic deliveries:

747-219B	5 (RB.211)

MALAYSIAN AIRLINES (H6)
First delivery: 12 March 1982

Malaysian Airlines now operates a large fleet of 747-400s powered both by the CF6 and the new PW4056 engine — but its 747 operations began in 1982 with a pair of 200-series aircraft built to a British Airways specification and powered by Rolls-Royce RB.211s. The two aircraft were already under construction when BA changed its mind about the order, and both were placed in storage for some months before attracting the attention of Malaysian Airlines. They were then reactivated and delivered to Kuala Lumpur in March and April 1982 as 9M-MHI and MHJ. The aircraft carried passengers for more than a decade, before both were converted into freighters during the mid-1990s. The only Classic ordered to a true Malaysian Airlines specification was a single 747-3H6 Combi, which was powered by JT9D engines and delivered in July 1986.

Total Classic deliveries:

747-236B	2 (RB.211)
747-3H6 Combi	1 (JT9D)

NIPPON AIR CARGO (81)
First delivery: 13 December 1984

As its name and Boeing customer-code suggests, Nippon Air Cargo (now called Nippon Cargo Airlines) is closely associated with — though not wholly owned by — All Nippon Airways. During the 1980s and early 1990s the carrier ordered six specialised 747-281F freighters, primarily for trans-Pacific routes between Tokyo and the United States. Since the start of opera-

LEFT: Saudi 747-368 HZ-AIO in the latest colour scheme. *Hugh Newell*

BELOW LEFT: Saudi 747-368 HZ-AIR still in the original colours. *Hugh Newell*

BELOW: Malaysian Airlines 747-3H6 Combi 9M-MHK.

tions in 1985 the route network has been expanded to include several points in Europe and Asia, and a much wider coverage of continental USA. To provide as much spares commonality as possible with All Nippon Airways, the cargo aircraft are all powered by CF6 engines.

Total Classic deliveries:

747-281F	6 (CF6)

MARTINAIR (1A)

First delivery: 23 February 1987

Martinair was founded as a family business in 1958 — equipped with a few light aircraft offering joy-rides and a limited number of very local charters. 30 years later it had grown into a worldwide charter airline, ready to add two brand new CF6-powered 747-21ACs to an existing fleet of DC-10s, A310s and MD-82s: the first aircraft was delivered in February 1987 and the second arrived at Schiphol in October 1988. Cargo and passenger charters could be operated with these convertible aircraft but to make things easier on the cargo side, both aircraft were fitted with the Boeing-designed side cargo door. During 1991 Martinair also took out a long-term lease on an ex-Air France 747-228F.

Total Classic deliveries:

747-21AC	2 (CF6)

EGYPTAIR (66)

First delivery: 22 June 1988

During 1984 Egyptair took out a short-term lease on a 747-257B powered by Pratt & Whitney JT9D engines: this ex-Swissair aircraft was allotted the registration SU-GAK but it stayed with the airline for less than a year. At the beginning of 1988 an order for two 747-366 Combis was announced and the first aircraft (SU-GAL) arrived in Cairo on 22 June that year. It was introduced into service on the Cairo–New York and Cairo–Tokyo routes and was joined by its sister-ship during the following month. Both aircraft were operated profitably for ten years, but when the first of Egyptair's Airbus A340s was delivered, SU-GAL was leased out to Royal Air Maroc. At the time of writing SU-GAM remains in service, but its days with Egyptair are probably numbered.

Total Classic deliveries:

747-366 Combi	2 (JT9D)

TOP LEFT: Nippon Cargo Airlines 747-281F Combi JA8172. *Geoff Harber*

CENTRE LEFT: The Oman Royal Flight's ex-Braniff 747-SP27 (A40-SP). *Hugh Newell*

ABOVE LEFT: The last SP ever built, the UAE's A40-SO.

LEFT: UAE 747-SP31. *Hugh Newell*

JAPAN ASIA AIRWAYS (46)

First delivery: 18 October 1988

The formation of Japan Asia Airways was a diplomatic manoeuvre to allow its Japan Air Lines parent to open up routes into China while continuing to serve Taiwan: the new company would operate solely to Taiwan, while JAL kept its hands clean and could be accepted into the People's Republic. The airline shares the same Boeing customer code (46) as its parent company and has often used its aircraft under various leasing agreements. Only one 747 has ever been purchased under the new name — a JT9D-powered 747-346 (JA8189), which was delivered during October 1988. The political situation in the region is now much more relaxed and Japan Asia's role has changed: in addition to the Taiwan services, it now operates to many other Asian destinations and offers scheduled-services support to its parent.

Total Classic deliveries:

747-346   1 (JT9D)

UNITED ARAB EMIRATES GOVERNMENT (Z5)

First delivery: 9 December 1989

The VIP fleet of member states of the United Arab Emirates consists of some of the most exotic personal transports in the world — none more so than the three 747-SPs operated by the Royal Flights of Dubai and Abu Dhabi. The first aircraft into service was an ex-TWA, JT9D-powered 747-SP31, which was bought by the Government of Dubai at the beginning of 1985.

This was followed by a purpose-built example ordered by the government of Abu Dhabi — which later proved to be the last 747SP ever built. This Rolls-Royce-powered aircraft was assembled at Everett some five years after the production of 'normal' 747-SPs had ceased: it was fitted with a substantial amount of quasi-military equipment (including sophisticated defences against air-to-air missile attack and an advanced satellite-communications system). The modification programme kept it on the ground for nearly two years after the first flight-tests of the basic airframe and published records show that it was finally delivered to the sheikdom during December 1989.

The last aircraft in the fleet was another ex-TWA 747-SP31: this was withdrawn from storage in 1993 and renovated and modified by Boeing to the same luxury standards as the original. All three of these aircraft are regular visitors to UK airports.

Total Classic deliveries:

747-SPZ5   1 (RB.211)

The buyers of new 747 Classics have been highlighted in this chapter: of course, there have been hundreds of second-hand or leased aircraft. At right are four examples.

TOP RIGHT: MASKargo 747-236B 9H-MHI. *Richard Potts*

CENTRE RIGHT: American International Airways 747-146SCD N702CK. *Geoff Harber*

ABOVE RIGHT: Air Atlanta TF-ABW.

RIGHT: Fiji-based Air Pacific DQ-FJE. *Geoff Harber*

7 ACCIDENTS AND INCIDENTS

The following chronological list shows details of all fatal accidents and incidents involving Classic 747s, together with a number of incidents that resulted in remarkable escapes for all on board.

30 July 1971
Pan American 747-100 N747PA

This was the first major incident involving a 747. It clearly demonstrated the enormous basic strength of the airframe, together with the success of its remarkable control-system redundancy: many a lesser aircraft would have crashed after receiving such damage, but the Pan Am crew managed to carry out a safe landing. The aircraft had been attempting to take-off from San Francisco International Airport, when it struck the approach lighting towers on the upwind end of the runway. The impact forced parts of the starboard inner undercarriage truck up into the cabin, injuring at least twenty passengers, some of them seriously: the primary structure and hydraulic and electrical systems were all severely damaged. An on-board doctor and the cabin staff treated the injured passengers, while the flight crew dumped fuel and organised an air-to-air inspection of the damage by a US Coast Guard aircraft. After nearly an hour in the air the crippled 747 landed back at San Francisco, but veered off the runway and came to rest with its nosewheel off the ground. There was no fire, and most of the passengers evacuated the aircraft by using the escape slides.

20 November 1974
Lufthansa 747-100 D-ABYB

The first fatal accident to a 747 occurred at Nairobi, as this Lufthansa aircraft attempted to take-off for the final leg of a routine Frankfurt to Johannesburg service. The aircraft stalled at about 200ft and fell back onto the runway with the landing gear unlocked at the beginning of its retraction sequence. After overrunning the upwind end of the runway, the rear fuselage hit an embankment and the aircraft began to break up, with the major portion coming to rest some 4,000ft beyond the end of the runway. There was no immediate fire and passengers started to evacuate from the starboard side of the fuselage: fire did, however, take hold just 30sec later and rapidly overwhelmed most of the aircraft. Of the 157 people on board, 57 passengers and two cabin crew were killed.

The subsequent enquiry blamed the cockpit crew. The flight engineer had failed to open the air-bleed valves after engine start, thus denying pressure to the aircraft's pneumatic system. The leading-edge slats of a 747 are normally deployed automatically (no separate crew-action needed) as part of the trailing-edge flap selection sequence prior to take-off. As soon as the flaps begin to move, the pneumatic slat-actuators begin

BELOW: The first 747 incident took place on 30 July 1971 and involved Pan Am's N747PA — luckily no one was killed as the aircraft showed remarlable durability. This is N533PA.

to expand, pushing the various slat groups forward and down, ahead of the wing leading-edge. The flight engineer's station has eight amber lights to show slats in motion, and eight green lights to show slats fully extended: the pilots have a single pair of amber/green lights to confirm the full movement and deployment of all slat groups. In the case of a clean wing (slats neither moving nor fully deployed), all the relevant lights on both panels are extinguished. In addition to the actual slat lights, a set of four amber lights tell the flight engineer that the engine bleed-air valves are closed and a gauge on the engineer's panel indicates the pressure (zero in this case) in the pneumatic-system duct.

On the day of the accident, the co-pilot (the designated handling pilot for that sector) called the *After Start* check list, which included verification that the bleed-air valve switches had been selected to 'open': the flight engineer called the *Taxiing* check list, which included a confirmation that the leading-edge slats were correctly set for take-off.

Despite these two separate checks, the crew failed to identify the problem, and lined up on the runway in a potentially dangerous configuration: when the aircraft rotated it was already in a semi-stalled condition and opening the big undercarriage doors (at the start of the retraction sequence) generated more drag than the wing could handle.

During the investigation of this accident it was revealed that several airline crews had had similar experiences with the 747, and that the regulatory authorities had been informed on at least two occasions under the mandatory incident reporting scheme. Some of these earlier incidents were almost 'rehearsals' for the Nairobi disaster, and yet nothing was done because they were considered to be isolated occurrences that would not overwhelm a properly co-ordinated crew. After Nairobi things were seen differently: leading edge slats were added to the stall-warning and take-off configuration warning systems, and the report recommended that non-operation (for whatever reason) of the take-off configuration warning system should become a 'no-go' item.

9 May 1976
Imperial Iranian AF 747-100F 5-283

This converted passenger aircraft (ex-N53111 of TWA) broke-up in mid-air over central Spain, while carrying cargo to the USAF base at Torrejon: the 17-man crew were all killed. Despite an extensive investigation no positive cause was ever established, but a number of clues strongly suggested a fuel explosion in the left wing — possibly caused by a lightning strike. The accident certainly occurred without warning during a violent thunderstorm, and the left wing tip — which was found several miles away from main crash site — showed no signs of fatigue or impact (possible collision) damage. US Government chemists examined fuel residues from the wreckage and found that the aircraft had probably been using the old military-standard Jet-B (JP4) wide-cut gasoline, instead of the recommended kerosene-based Jet-A commercial fuel: the ullage of Jet-B is known to be highly-explosive under certain conditions and a lightning discharge could have provided the source

of ignition. In the absence of proof, the US Federal Aviation Agency issued an Airworthiness Directive to 747 operators, requiring them to check all the dry bays within the wing and engine pylons for evidence of fuel leaks. Nothing was found and it was therefore assumed that the suggestion of a lightning strike was the most likely explanation. The original investigation was closed on this slightly unsatisfactory note, but renewed interest is now being shown in the accident because of its similarity to the equally unexplained destruction of a TWA 747 in July 1996 (see below).

27 March 1977
KLM 747-200 PH-BUF/Pan American 747-100 N736PA

The head-on collision between these two aircraft on the runway at Tenerife's Los Rodeos airport was the ultimate aviation nightmare. The facts of the case are horribly clear, but a realistic assessment of why it was allowed to happen is less obvious.

A terrorist bomb explosion in the terminal building had caused nearby Las Palmas Airport to be closed and this generated widespread disruption to planned air traffic in the area. A number of flights (including the Pan Am and KLM 747s) were diverted to Tenerife and these rapidly filled all the available parking slots — and some of the taxiways — at Los Rodeos, putting considerable pressure on normal ground movements: these problems were made worse by drifting low cloud in the area, which had reduced the runway visual range to 300m just four minutes before the crash.

After refuelling for its direct flight to Amsterdam, the KLM aircraft was asked to backtrack down the full length of the runway and turn to await take-off clearance. The Pan Am aircraft, meanwhile, had been given clearance to follow KLM, and '*leave the runway third, third on your left*' (referring to the third of four exit points, which would have put the Pan Am on a taxiway parallel to the runway). Turn-3 was an acute (146-degree) left turn onto a diagonal link between the runway and the taxiway, to be followed by a similar right-hand turn to arrive on the taxiway itself. Such turns are difficult to see in poor visibility and not easy to accomplish at any time in a heavily loaded 747. For whatever reason, the Pan Am crew missed this turning and continued down the runway towards Turn-4. At only 34-degrees, this exit was much more easily seen from a 747 cockpit and would have been a more logical route to give such a big aircraft.

By this time the KLM aircraft had reached the end of the runway and turned, and was awaiting final take-off and ATC clearances. These were both requested in one sentence and the tower responded with a sentence beginning '*KLM 8705, you are cleared to the Papa Alpha beacon*' and continuing with the Air Traffic instructions that would see them safely out of the area and heading for Las Palmas VOR at 9,000ft: no specific take-off clearance had been given, but the KLM crew interpreted the message as meaning that they could take-off and climb to FL90. While the captain released the brakes and began the take-off roll, the first officer read back the ATC instructions, and added the slightly ambiguous '*we are now ah — taking off*', or possibly '*we are now at take-off.*'

The tower interpreted this message as meaning that KLM was at the take-off position and awaiting clearance and replied by saying 'OK. (a pause for nearly two seconds, and then) Stand by for take-off....I will call you.' In fact the aircraft was already accelerating towards the unseen Pan Am 747, which was still shrouded in fog and invisible from both the tower and the KLM cockpit. The first signs of alarm came from the Pan Am crew, who heard the KLM/tower conversation and intervened with confirmation that they were still on the runway. The tower (believing that KLM was still awaiting clearance), asked Pan Am to report as soon as the runway was clear. This exchange was picked up in the KLM cockpit, but too late to avoid the collision. The Pan Am crew saw the lights of the KLM aircraft only nine seconds before impact: they tried to turn off the runway, but the KLM's undercarriage and rear fuselage smashed into the cabin roof of their aircraft. The KLM captain had tried to avoid the collision by over-rotating on take-off (tail-scrape scars were found on the runway surface), and turning away from the obvious point of impact. The two aircraft finally came to rest about 450m apart, both burning fiercely. Remarkably, nine crew and 61 passengers of the Pan Am aircraft survived, but everyone on board the KLM aircraft perished.

The Spanish report firmly blamed the Dutch captain for taking-off without positive clearance: it also cited the Pan Am crew as a major contributory cause, by not using Turn-3 as instructed and not confirming to the tower that they had missed it. The report disappointed the whole aviation community: it seemed far more concerned with deflecting blame from all things Spanish, than it was in considering valuable safety issues — in particular, the ambiguous phraseology used by Air Traffic Control. The Dutch crew had all been killed and the Pan Am crew were not even called to give evidence to the enquiry — other than a brief interview less than 48 hours after the crash actually happened.

1 January 1978
Air India 747-200 VT-EBD
This aircraft took-off in darkness at 8.09pm (local) from Bombay's Santa Cruz airport, bound for Dubai with 23 crew and 190 passengers on board. Just 101 seconds later it crashed into the Arabian Sea, with its wings 18-degrees past the vertical and its nose down at an angle of 35-degrees: everyone on board was killed.

Things started to go wrong at about 1,400ft, when the captain began to straighten-up after a climbing right-hand turn to intercept his departure radial. At this point his mechanical ADI (Attitude Director Indicator — in simple terms his artificial horizon) failed, but without displaying its 'failure' flag. In order to level the wings against what he perceived as a gentle right-handed bank, the captain applied increasing amounts of left-handed aileron, until the aircraft reached an extreme attitude, from which it could not recover in the height available. The co-pilot — whose ADI display was powered separately and stabilised by a different inertial platform — failed to notice (or failed to tell the captain) that the aircraft's attitude was way outside the normal range, until it was far too late to do anything

about it. Even without the co-pilot's warning, the captain should have been aware of the problem after scanning the rest of his instruments, which included a standby artificial horizon.

After identifying a lack of crew co-ordination as the major cause of the accident, the official report went on to make a number of recommendations about specific aspects of crew training and crew examination procedures.

19 November 1980
Korean Airlines 747-200 HL7445
This accident occurred while the aircraft was landing in early morning fog at Seoul's Kimpo International Airport. The flight was inbound from Los Angeles (via Anchorage), with 226 people on board. It was low on approach and touched down some distance short of the paved runway, and was reported to have 'hit a barrier' (believed to be a military anti-aircraft gun emplacement), which effectively destroyed the main undercarriage trucks. On the runway, it collapsed onto its nosewheel and belly, and slid for nearly a mile before catching fire — possibly because the centre-wing tank had been ruptured by the initial impact. The emergency evacuation chutes were deployed remarkably quickly, and 213 people escaped from the aircraft. All three flight crew and several of the cabin staff died in the fire. The subsequent report blamed the pilots for misjudging their approach.

23 July 1982
British Airways 747-200 G-BDXH
This aircraft had a remarkable escape after all four of the Rolls-Royce RB.211 engines failed within minutes of each other, as it flew through a cloud of volcanic ash and dust at cruising altitude. Flying between Kuala Lumpur and Perth with 16 crew and 236 passengers on board, it ran into trouble about 100nm south of Jakarta, at 20.45hr (local). Mount Gallungung, a volcano in southern Sumatra, had been erupting spasmodically for several months, but on that night it suffered a huge explosion that blew a plume of pulverised rock particles into the air, reaching an altitude of well over 45,000ft. The 747 was cruising at FL370 (37,000ft) and the sky was already very dark: the cloud of dust could not be seen and it was totally invisible to the weather-radar, so the aircraft just blundered into it without any warning.

The first real sign of trouble was a curious St Elmo's Fire effect around the exposed surfaces of the airframe, which became particularly concentrated around the engines. In the total darkness of the night these appeared to glow brightly, with an intense white light emanating from behind the big front fans — giving the impression of four forward-facing floodlights (it was later realised that this light was created by billions of sparks, each generated by a tiny piece of pumice-like rock hitting the rapidly rotating metal surfaces). There was no external noise to accompany the phenomenon and the crew was still trying to work out what it was, when No.4 engine failed without any warning. They had just completed the fire drill and shutdown procedure for No.4, when No.2 failed, rapidly followed by the other two. They were now in a 400-ton glider, miles

ABOVE: Thirteen people died when Korean Airlines HL7445 (seen here in 1979) crash-landed at Seoul's Kimpo airport in November 1980.

from anywhere, with no generators, and with a diminishing amount of standby power to run all the aircraft systems and instrumentation: they were also still in the dust cloud.

An emergency was called (Jakarta Control responded) and engine re-light procedures were initiated, starting with those straight from 'the book', and then trying anything that might work — including going well beyond the recommended speed range for an in-flight start. Dozens of re-light attempts were made and the aircraft had lost nearly 24,000ft before No.4 finally started: the aircraft had been without power of any kind for 13 minutes. Although lacking its full thrust, this one engine restored some electrical services and allowed the crew to slow their rate of descent. Over the next few minutes the three remaining engines started, but No.2 suffered repeated surges and had to be shut down completely.

The landing at Jakarta was far from easy. Aircraft speed had to be controlled mainly by air brakes, because the engines were all badly damaged by erosion and were very sensitive to throttle changes. The volcanic ash had sand-blasted most of the for-ward-facing surfaces of the aircraft — so the windscreens were largely opaque, and the landing-lights were so diffused that they were virtually useless. To cap it all, the ILS glide-slope was inoperative on that day, which ruled out any chance of an automatic landing.

In the event, the captain discovered a small section of rela-tively clear glass on the lower left-hand edge of his windscreen, and this enabled him to see the Visual Approach Slope Indicators on his side of the runway. For their initial approach, the crew used the ILS localiser (which was working normally)

and monitored their descent using DME. Later — as the air-craft got closer to the ground — the captain maintained his lim-ited view of the VASIs, the co-pilot monitored the radio altime-ter and called out every 25ft, while the flight engineer called out the speeds. Under the circumstances the whole approach and touchdown went remarkably well and was an enormous relief after serious consideration had been given to the possibility of a midnight ditching.

31 August 1983
Korean Airlines 747-200 HL7442

The destruction of this aircraft caused world-wide diplomatic anger because it was cold-bloodedly shot down by the Soviet Air Force, with the loss of 269 innocent lives. The aircraft had been operating a regular scheduled service between New York and Seoul and had stopped at Anchorage for fuel and a fresh crew. During the final leg of this journey the pilots allowed their course to stray considerably north of the planned route, and unwittingly made landfall over Soviet military areas on the Kamchatka Peninsula (instead of the planned overflight of the Japanese island of Hokkaido): still unaware of their situation, they then continued over the Sea of Okhostk towards a highly sensitive missile-testing facility on the island of Sakhalin. According to official Soviet sources, up to eight fighters were involved at one time or another in the interception and shadow-ing operation, and all the pilots thought the so-called 'target' was a US Air Force RC-135 reconnaissance aircraft — appar-ently none of them recognised it as a commercial jet, despite being in close contact with it for over an hour and reporting that it was flying with strobe and navigation lights on. Attempted radio contacts were unsuccessful, and after allegedly firing four bursts of tracer-ammunition as a final warning, one of the accompanying Sukhoi Su-15 *Flagon* fighters launched a salvo of two AA-3 *Anab* missiles: the aircraft was hit at 18.26 GMT (03.26 local), and crashed into a Soviet-controlled area of the Sea of Japan.

Exactly what happened on the Korean flightdeck will never be known, but later analysis suggested a sequence of events that matches all the known facts. On departure, the aircraft was routed to join Jetway 501 to Bethel VOR, on a heading of 239 degrees: this stage would probably have been flown with the autopilot in *heading reference* mode. At Bethel, the heading should have changed slightly to 237 degrees, and the autopilot mode should have been changed to *Nav*, bringing the INS into play. If that autopilot change had not been made (or if the rotary mode-control switch had failed to operate correctly), the aircraft would have remained on its previously set heading of 239 degrees and all off-track warnings would have been suppressed. Nevertheless, the pilots were clearly not paying attention.

27 November 1983
Avianca 747-200C HK-2910X

Early versions of the Ground Proximity Warning System (GPWS) could give an irritating number of false warnings — so much so that a number of pilots ignored, or blatantly disbelieved, its strident demands for caution. This Avianca 747 was on a night approach to Madrid's Barajas Airport, as one of the planned stops on a scheduled Frankfurt to Bogota service. It was far lower on finals than it should have been and eventually hit an area of level ground about four nautical miles south-east of the runway: despite being in a stable, flat attitude, the aircraft was totally destroyed. Of the 194 people on board, only 11 passengers survived. It was later discovered that the altimeters had been incorrectly set. The GPWS had sounded its '*Pull up. Pull up.*' warning just 15 sec before impact, but the last intelligible sound heard on the cockpit voice recorder was an unknown member of the crew saying '*Shut up Gringo.*'

19 February 1985
China Airlines 747SP N4522V

While cruising at 41,000ft this aircraft suddenly rolled violently to the right, and entered an uncontrolled dive that was not recovered until it had reached 9,500ft: considerable structural damage was done to the horizontal stabilisers and elevators, but only two people were seriously injured.

The aircraft was *en route* from Taipei to Los Angeles with 274 people on board — and was 300nm off San Francisco when it ran into trouble. The autopilot was flying the aircraft, in daylight (about 10.00hr local) and at Mach 0.85, when the flight encountered the kind of moderate turbulence associated with entering a jetstream. Windshear then generated airspeed fluctuations between Mach 0.84 and Mach 0.88, and the autopilot tried to maintain its programmed number by using the autothrottle system. One of the engines (No.4 — the starboard outer) was lagging behind the others because of a minor fault in the fuel system and the flight engineer tried to restore parity by manually retarding the throttle and then slowly advancing it

again. Unfortunately he forgot to close the engine's bleed-air valves — which caused a flame-out, creating asymmetric thrust and further speed decay. The captain should have taken manual control of the aircraft at that point, but instead he continued to rely on the autopilot and tried to correct the speed decay by selecting nose-down pitch on the autopilot control wheel. While he was concentrating solely on the airspeed problem, asymmetric thrust had taken hold of the aircraft and generated a significant (23°) roll to the right. When the autopilot was finally disengaged, the immediate effects took the crew by surprise — the existing levels of bank and nose-down pitch rapidly developed into a full-scale nose-over and vertical dive. Control was eventually recovered and the aircraft landed safely, but the degree of structural damage amazed Boeing engineers.

23 June 1985
Air India 747-200 VT-EFO

Because of its great size and obvious news value, the 747 has often been the target of terrorism. This Air India aircraft was at cruising altitude over the Atlantic, about 50 miles from the west-coast of Ireland, when it was brought down by a large bomb in the forward luggage hold. The flight had originated in Canada and was on its way to Bombay, via London, when it suddenly disappeared from the radar screens of Shannon's oceanic area control centre: all 329 people on board were killed. The crash caused considerable anxiety in the airline industry, because the immediate cause was unknown and any major fatigue-failure could have had the same catastrophic effect as a bomb. The wreckage had to examined — and quickly, but it was lying in 6,700ft of water and spread along a trail at least seven miles long. A huge international effort managed to recover more than 20% of the aircraft, with each piece taking up to 18hr to bring to the surface. The flight data recorder and cockpit voice recorder were recovered intact, but as expected they showed nothing unusual until the moment they both ceased operating — presumably through lack of electrical power caused by the initial break-up. The wreckage analysis failed to offer conclusive evidence of a bomb, but it also suggested that fatigue could be ruled out. A painstaking investigation of all the circumstances surrounding the aircraft's departure (baggage inter-lining records, passenger no-shows, lack of refund claims for certain unused tickets, and the failure to make insurance claims for unaccompanied baggage, etc) created a compelling circumstantial case for the sabotage theories. On the same day as the Air India disaster, an attempt was made to bomb a CP Air flight originating in Vancouver and bound for Tokyo's Narita Airport. The aircraft landed safely, but as the baggage was being unloaded a bomb exploded in one of the suitcases, killing two of the airport staff and seriously injuring six others: had it gone off in the air, it would certainly have destroyed the aircraft.

19 August 1985
Japan Airlines 747SR JA8119

The loss of this short-range variant of the 747 claimed the lives of 520 passengers and crew, which continues to be the world's worst air disaster involving just a single aircraft. Flight JL123 took-off from Tokyo's Haneda Airport at 18.12 (local), to begin the 45min domestic sector to Osaka, about 150 miles to the south-west of Tokyo. Twelve minutes later, just as the aircraft reached its assigned altitude of 24,000ft, the 4.55m diameter rear bulkhead suddenly ruptured, allowing all the pressurised cabin air to escape into the unpressurised tail section of the fuselage. Most of this excess pressure went straight up into the hollow tail fin, which inflated like a balloon and burst: the 450kt airflow then carried 50% of the fin structure (and both rudder sections) away, with debris falling into the sea about 95 miles from the final crash site.

The pilots, meanwhile, knew very little about the severity of the damage. They were aware of the rapid decompression at 18.24hr, but thought the starboard rear passenger door had failed (the cockpit warning light for this door had illuminated, but probably as a result of structural distortion). The crew immediately asked for permission to return to Haneda, but the effectiveness of all flight controls degraded very rapidly until, at 18.47hr, the flight engineer announced that all hydraulic pressure in all four systems had been lost. The aircraft then wandered the skies at random, with all pilot control inputs having no effect whatsoever. An attempt was made to control the aircraft by using engine thrust alone, but the capacity to do this was very limited without the pitch-changing advantages of a trijet-style tail engine: the alternative (electrical) operation of the main flap groups was tried briefly, but any extension was a slow process and carried with it an extreme risk of stalling. By this time the aircraft's random manoeuvres had taken it over an area of mountainous terrain and its natural stability was being rocked by mountain winds and updraughts: with each turn it lost speed and altitude, until at 18.56hr — just 32min after the bulkhead failure — it crashed into a heavily forested hillside some 70 miles north west of Tokyo. Remarkably, four of the passengers survived.

It was later confirmed that this particular aircraft had been involved in a heavy tail-impact landing during 1978: 30 passengers had been injured on that occasion and the airframe suffered considerable damage. A team of Boeing engineers had been called in to conduct on-site repairs, but work on the bulkhead had not been carried out correctly, with the result that it weakened with time and eventually failed along the original repair line: all four of the aircraft's hydraulic systems pass through the bulkhead and up into the tail, and when it burst with such severity, all four were ruptured.

5 September 1986
Pan American 747-100 N656PA

Another casualty of terrorism, this aircraft was hijacked at Karachi by four Palestine Liberation Organisation gunmen, who demanded to be flown to Cyprus in order to secure the release of PLO prisoners on the island. As soon as the gunmen came aboard, the flight crew abandoned the aircraft through a hatch in the cockpit roof and escaped down a rope. This effectively immobilised the aircraft for 17 hours, while the airport authorities brought an Arabic-speaking crew in from Frankfurt

(this was simply a delaying tactic on the part of the security forces). Negotiations with Pan Am and Government officials seemed to be making progress, when the aircraft's auxiliary power unit (APU) suddenly stopped working and all the lights went out: at this point the hijackers suspected a deliberate trick and opened fire indiscriminately inside the cabin — killing 18 passengers and seriously wounding about 100 others. In fact, the APU had simply stopped because the tank it was coupled to had run out of fuel.

28 November 1987
South African Airways 747-200B ZS-SAS

This South African Airways Combi aircraft was en route to Johannesburg from Taipei, with a planned fuel stop in Mauritius. About 140 miles from Mauritius, the captain asked for an emergency descent from cruise altitude to 14,000ft: he reported a fire on board and smoke in the cockpit. A few minutes after receiving descent clearance he gave a full position report, and then confirmed that the aircraft was losing a lot of its on-board electrical systems. Mauritius only had time to confirm straight-in clearances and receive a brief acknowledgement, before all contact was lost. The aircraft crashed into the Indian Ocean — possibly breaking up before impact. There were no survivors among the 160 people on board.

The wreckage was found in 14,500ft of water. It was remotely photographed and mapped in some detail, but only a small quantity of it was ever recovered — although most of that had been specially-targeted after examining the photographs and video record of the crash scene. The flight data recorder was never found: the cockpit voice recorder was recovered, but not until January 1989 and by then most of the tape was too indistinct to be of any use.

It was clear from the recovered wreckage that the fire had started in the aft main-deck cargo compartment. No clues as to the origin of the fire could be found, but it was obvious that the number of extinguishers on board was inadequate and metallurgical examination suggested that temperatures of at least 1,000°C had been generated before the aircraft hit the sea. Thermal pressure had built up in the semi-sealed cargo compartment and this had finally burst through the ceiling in the galley area, allowing smoke and toxic fumes to enter the main deck passenger cabin.

The implications of this accident had a profound effect on aviation-safety authorities all over the world — and for a while, the whole concept of Combi operations was threatened. The system of accepting large containers — full of unknown, possibly inflammable or toxic cargo — onto passenger aircraft was fraught with previously unseen dangers. To avoid a repeat of the disaster, a comprehensive raft of new regulations were introduced to ensure the safety all Combi-style aircraft — not just the 747. The new rules included the fire-hardening of the aircraft themselves; the training of cabin crews to deal with on-board fires; the carriage of adequate fire-fighting tools and equipment; and the monitoring of cargo areas for early signs of smoke and high temperatures.

5 April 1988
Kuwait Airways 747-200 9K-ADA
This aircraft was subjected to one of the longest hijackings in aviation history. Eight members of the Shiite group *Islamic Jihad* boarded the aircraft at Bangkok, armed with hand grenades and automatic weapons. Soon after take-off they assumed control and demanded to be taken to Mashhad — in NE Iran — where the group's leader came on board carrying more guns and explosives. The aircraft was refuelled, but the Iranian authorities blocked the runway and refused to let it leave: after a two-day stand-off, 57 non-Kuwaiti passengers were released and the aircraft was allowed to depart for an unknown destination. As soon as it was airborne it made for Beirut, but the authorities there also blocked the runway with vehicles — this time to prevent it landing. The aircraft circled Beirut for three hours, until desperate pleas from the pilot about his dangerously low fuel state were picked up by the Cypriot government and nearby Larnaca airport was opened up — apparently as a humanitarian gesture. During the following few days all demands for fuel were refused, until first one and then another of the hostages were shot dead and unceremoniously dumped from the aircraft in full view of the world's media: threats to kill again were taken seriously, and the aircraft was eventually refuelled for what was to become the final leg of its journey — to Algiers. After many more tedious hours of negotiation on the tarmac at Algiers, the hostages finally woke up on the morning of 20 April to find themselves alone: the hijackers had made a deal with the Algerian authorities and had been spirited away to a secret destination in exchange for the lives of their remaining captives. The hijack had lasted for 15 days, cost the lives of two men, and achieved nothing.

21 December 1988
Pan American 747-100 N739PA
The destruction of Pan Am's Flight 103 proved to be a landmark in the battle against terrorism — mainly because the wreckage fell on the small Scottish town of Lockerbie. This made it possible to carry out an immediate and thorough investigation, but it also provided the newspaper and TV people with some unforgettable images — which spurred political action on both sides of the Atlantic (the earlier bombing of an Air India 747 occurred over the sea and did not have the same shock value to those who were not directly involved).

Flight PA103 originated in Frankfurt and it seems that the suitcase containing the bomb cleared security there and was loaded into a container for onward transmission to London and New York: the first leg of the journey was flown in a Pan Am Boeing 727. Many more passengers joined the Flight in London and the type of aircraft was (as planned) switched to a 747. All the London passengers and their bags had been through the Heathrow security system, but the Frankfurt-based baggage was already considered to be secure and was simply loaded aboard without additional checks.

The flight took-off slightly late and was routinely passed from London Air Traffic Control Centre, to Scottish, and then to the Oceanic Centre, and had been established at its initial cruise altitude of 31,000ft for seven minutes. At just after 19.00hr (local), the transponder signature disappeared from the controller's radar screen and all contact was lost: the radar tapes then show that the aircraft broke into five major sections, and began to fall over a huge area of open country, mainly to the east of the A74 Carlisle to Glasgow road. All 16 crew and 243 passengers were killed. The heavy, fuel-laden wing and some of the engines (all of which had separated during the descent) fell into a residential area of Lockerbie, instantly demolishing several houses and drenching others in burning jet fuel. Eleven people died on the ground and more were injured. Had the aircraft left on schedule, it would have fallen into the Atlantic.

In total, the wreckage was scattered over an area of more than 700 square miles and it took a huge military operation lasting many weeks to gather it all together. Within a few days of the crash, the Farnborough-based UK Air Accident Investigation Branch had found explosive residues on the metal framework of one of the baggage containers, and painstaking scientific analysis later revealed that about 1kg of Semtex high-performance plastic explosive had been concealed in a cheap radio/cassette player, which in turn had been hidden in an unsuspecting passenger's luggage. Conventional police work then took over and after an exhaustive investigation two suspects were named — both Libyan nationals. Both deny the charges. Sanctions and a long period of international diplomacy were needed to finally secure their arrest, but at the time of writing the trial has yet to begin.

19 February 1989
Flying Tiger 747-200F N807FT
This aircraft was approaching Kuala Lumpur in bad weather at the end of a scheduled cargo flight from Singapore, when it simply disappeared from the controller's radar screen. There were no distress calls and no earlier indications of any technical problem. It crashed into a hillside about seven miles short of the runway and most of the wreckage was consumed by an intense fire: all four crew members died.

The flight data recorder and cockpit voice recorder were both recovered intact and it was later discovered that the approach controller had used non-standard phraseology: the crew — misinterpreting the clearances given — had descended below safety height with fatal consequences.

24 February 1989
United Airlines 747-100 N4713U
In many ways this accident proved to be a remarkable escape for most of the 355 occupants, but nine passengers died and several more were injured by flying debris. The aircraft was climbing out of Honolulu at the start of a scheduled flight to Auckland, in New Zealand. About 20min after take-off — with the aircraft at about 23,000ft and some 70 miles into the ocean crossing — the forward cargo door on the starboard side flew open with such force that it tore a huge hole in the main-deck cabin wall above. The explosive decompression sucked nine passengers out of the cabin, left a hole 10ft wide by 20ft high in the forward fuselage structure, damaged part of the wing lead-

ing-edge, and caused No3 engine (the starboard inner) to fail after ingesting debris: there was also a fire in No4 (starboard outer) and that had to be shut down too. The crew called an emergency, dumped fuel, and managed to make it back to Honolulu for a safe landing after just over an hour in the air.

It was a relief that the aircraft had remained flyable after sustaining such damage, but the implications of a sudden door failure were all too clear — especially for operators of high-time 747s. All the debris had fallen into 16,000ft of water and the recovery of vital evidence seemed unlikely. An examination of the aircraft itself quickly discounted a bomb, corrosion or fatigue failure as possible causes, which left faulty operation of the latching mechanism or inadequate maintenance as the two most likely candidates.

About a year before this accident, a similar — though less serious — incident occurred when the same type of door partially opened in flight on a Pan American aircraft. The FAA then issued an Airworthiness Directive (AD) requiring that certain inspections and modifications be carried out — the modifications to be completed within two years, or earlier if the inspection deemed necessary: this particular United aircraft had been inspected but not yet modified. As a result of this second door failure, the AD modification programme was accelerated and all 747 door latches had to be strengthened within 30 days: additional checks of in-service aircraft were also ordered, and new rules were introduced to ensure the safe operation of all cargo doors.

The full accident report published by the US National Transportation Safety Board in April 1990 criticised the FAA, Boeing and United Airlines for their lack of timely action following the earlier Pan Am incident: it went on to imply that the United aircraft's door was not properly latched on departure, and it criticised its maintenance and inspection procedures.

Against all expectations, the cargo door was located and recovered by the US Navy — but not until September 1990. After examining the latch mechanism, the NTSB exonerated United Airlines and issued a revised set of findings. These suggested that faulty wiring or electrical components in the door operating mechanism had triggered 'an uncommanded electrical actuation of the door' (locking cams) — probably during ground operations immediately before take-off. The criticisms of the FAA and Boeing were not retracted from the later report.

29 December 1991
China Airlines 747-200F B-198
The captain of this cargo aircraft reported engine trouble shortly after take-off and asked for immediate clearance to return to Taipei. It was originally thought that he had reported the failure of No2 (port inner) engine. The aircraft was on its way back to the airport when all contact was lost: wreckage was later found in mountainous terrain about 11nm (20km) north-east of Taipei. All five crew were killed. The weather at the time (15.00 local) was reported as poor visibility in drizzly rain.

Much of the wreckage was deeply embedded in the damp, mountain soil and it took several weeks to recover the majority of it: only then did the investigation team realise that the two starboard engines (numbers 3 and 4) could not be found at the crash scene. It soon became evident that they had separated in flight and possibly fallen into the sea: if this was so, the pilot's initial report of the incident probably referred to the loss of *two* engines, rather than the loss of *number 2* (which was found at the crash site, and appeared to working normally at the time of impact). Based on a computed flight-path for the aircraft, the search was switched to a huge area of the South China Sea. Engine No.4 was found in February 1992 and internal scoring and fire damage led the team to believe that this engine had, indeed, failed in flight. Engine No.3 was not found until July: this was operating normally up to the point of separation, but its mounting assembly was missing, which provided the first real clue as to what had happened. The search for the mounting continued, but in the meantime Boeing engineers issued a service bulletin, advising operators to inspect the main spar fuse pins (a vital part of the engine mounting assembly) on all early 747s. Just six weeks later, an El Al cargo aircraft crashed in remarkably similar circumstances.

4 October 19992
El Al 747-200F 4X-AXG
Like the China Airlines aircraft mentioned above, this was a dedicated freighter that lost both of its starboard engines during climb-out after an uneventful take-off. The starboard inner (No.3) detached first, and this then hit the outer engine on the same wing (No.4) with such force that it too separated a few seconds later. Most of the leading-edge devices on the starboard wing sustained considerable damage, as did the hydraulic and pneumatic systems.

The aircraft had taken-off at 18.21 (local) from Amsterdam's Schiphol Airport, *en route* to Tel Aviv with three crew, one company passenger and a full load of cargo on board. Six minutes later it was climbing normally through about 6,500ft when a fire warning was triggered for No.3 engine, followed three of four seconds later by another for engine No.4. The Captain — believing that both engines had simply failed and lost power — declared an emergency and attempted to return to Schiphol: he was not aware at that stage that the engines had actually fallen off, or that his flight controls on the starboard wing had been damaged. He initiated a right turn and began to dump fuel in preparation for the landing, but was forced to reduce power on the port engines to counteract the strong asymmetric forces. As soon as he did this, the aircraft began to lose speed and height, and threatened to stall. Landing flap settings were selected in an attempt to gain more lift, but the starboard groups failed to function properly and the port wing lifted, pitching the aircraft into a spiral dive from which it could not recover. At 18.33 (local) the pilot reported control problems, followed at 18.36 by the message 'We are going down'. A few seconds later the aircraft rolled 90° to the vertical and crashed into a large apartment block on the outskirts of Amsterdam: all four occupants of the aircraft were killed, together with about 70 people on the ground.

The Netherlands Accident Investigation Bureau report was published in April 1994. It confirmed that the El Al aircraft had suffered a fatigue failure of one of the No.3 engine's inboard mid-spar structural fuse pins. This had fractured at a time when the engine was at take-off power, putting undue stress on the remaining engine-mounting components: these had also progressively failed, causing the whole pylon and engine assembly to break away from the wing. The engine was still generating full power for a few seconds after separation (due to existing fuel in the lines), and it collided heavily with No.4, which was badly damaged by the side-impact loads and fell away a few seconds later. The departure of either or both of the engines damaged many of the high-lift systems on the starboard wing, making continued flight almost impossible.

This crash was clearly linked to the loss of the China Airlines aircraft in Dec 91 and later analysis of both accidents suggested the same root cause. Subsequent actions included modification and strengthening of all 747 engine mountings, and an FAA-mandated increase in both the frequency and thoroughness of fuse-pin inspections: these new procedures affected all early JT9D-powered 747s (some 470 aircraft), together with all Boeing 757 models — which have similar engine-mounting fuse-pins.

11 December 1994
Philippine Airlines 747-200 EI-BWF
This aircraft was *en route* from Cebu in the Philippines to Tokyo, with 20 crew and 287 passengers on board. One of the passengers detonated a small bomb in the cabin, killing himself and seriously injuring six other people: a large hole was blown in the passenger-cabin floor, and some ancillary damage was done, but the explosion did not breach the pressure shell or inflict major damage to any of the flight-critical systems. The aircraft immediately diverted to Naha Airport on the island of Okinawa, where the crew made a successful emergency landing.

17 July 1996
Trans World Airlines 747-100 N93119
A positive cause for the destruction of TWA's Flight 800 may never be known. The aircraft had taken-off from Kennedy Airport, New York, at 20.19hr (local), bound for Paris with 210 passengers and 18 crew on board: a few minutes later, as it was climbing through 13,000ft, it suffered a catastrophic in-flight explosion, causing it to break up instantly and fall into the sea just off the coast of Long Island. There were no survivors.

The wreckage fell into relatively shallow waters (about 100ft or so), and was found in two major debris fields some 1.5nm (2.4km) apart: it was therefore accessible to US Navy divers and most of it was ultimately recovered.

The suddenness of the break up led to a frenzy of speculation that a bomb had been involved. Several independent eye witnesses even claimed to have seen the exhaust trail of a surface-to-air missile streaking towards the aircraft, followed by a huge fireball in the night sky. The assumption of criminal or terrorist activity connected with the Atlanta Olympic Games (due to start just two days after the crash) was raised in the public mind and the FBI was brought into the investigation process. Sadly, the criminal investigation quickly assumed pri-

macy over the technical examination, which hampered and considerably delayed the work of the National Transportation Safety Board.

In their own investigation, members of the NTSB soon began to focus on the possibility of an explosion of volatile fuel vapours in the wing centre-section tank — caused either by an electrical short-circuit, or by high-velocity debris from an explosion in one of the inboard engines. Evidence from the recovered flight data recorder suggested that all four engines were running normally right up to the time of the explosion, and there was no sense of alarm or suggestion of a technical problem on the cockpit voice recorder tapes.

Despite an extensive search for chemical-explosive residues, none was found. The missile theory was examined in the greatest detail. No evidence was found of any kind of external blast damage, and the US Navy — which had been accused of mistakenly launching an inert drill round at the aircraft — had irrefutable records to show that the nearest warship was many miles away at the time and that no drill rounds had been fired during that evening. It soon became obvious that the explosion had occurred *inside* the centre wing tank, but the source of ignition remains to this day a complete mystery.

12 November 1996
Saudi Arabian Airlines 747-100 HZ-AIH
This aircraft was outbound from Indira Gandhi Airport, New Delhi, having just taken-off for Dhahran and Jeddah in Saudi Arabia, with 312 passengers and crew on board. At 17.40hr (local), only seven minutes after departure, the 747 collided head-on with an Il-76 (UN-76435) operated by Air Kazakhstan and inbound to the same airport. The Kazakh aircraft was carrying mainly cargo, but it also had 38 people on board: all 350 occupants of both aircraft were killed.

The Saudi aircraft had been cleared to FL140 (14,000ft), and was holding this altitude on a westerly track of 270° from the Delhi VOR beacon (DPN). The Ilyushin meanwhile, was inbound to DPN on a reciprocal course of 90°, but cleared only to '*descend and maintain FL150*' (15,000ft). The two should have passed each other vertically separated by 1,000ft, before the outbound aircraft resumed its climb, and the inbound its descent. For some reason the Kazakh pilot actually continued descending and levelled-off at FL140: he then reported to ATC that he was level at *FL150* and the collision became almost inevitable.

At that time the East/West arrival and departure tracks at New Delhi were not laterally separated, and ATC had to rely on individual crews maintaining an assigned altitude. To make matters worse, the airport was only equipped with a primary surveillance radar — which gives positional information but does not show altitude. The controller therefore had no independent check that the two aircraft were following his instructions. The ATC tapes show clear, unambiguous, requests and acknowledgements, so both pilots knew exactly what was expected of them: the Kazakh pilot was even told about the '*Identified traffic, 12 o'clock reciprocal*' at FL140, and asked to '*Report when in sight.*' A minute or so later the two aircraft collided, with the Ilyushin impacting the top of the 747. Neither aircraft was equipped with TCAS (Traffic-alert and Collision Avoidance System) — which would have given them adequate warning of the impending danger and a climb or descent instruction as a means of resolving the conflict.

The official report confirmed that the inbound Il-76 was 1,000ft lower than it should have been — possibly because its crew had failed to accurately convert its metric altimeter-reading to imperial. As a direct result of this accident, the Indian Government decided that TCAS would become a compulsory system for all passenger aircraft operating within Indian airspace. The New Delhi ATC system should, by now, have been upgraded with a new Secondary Surveillance Radar (SSR), which provides altitude and speed information, as well as individual aircraft identification.

6 August 1997
Korean Airlines 747-300 HL7468

This aircraft was making a night approach to runway 06L at Guam's Agana International Airport, when it hit high ground and broke up some 3nm (5.6km) from touchdown: virtually all of the passenger cabin was destroyed by the heavy impact and subsequent fire — but remarkably, 26 of the 254 occupants managed to survive.

This particular route was normally operated by KAL's fleet of Airbus A300-600s, but a few days earlier one of these aircraft had skidded off the runway during a domestic flight, sustaining damage and leaving the airline short of capacity. A 747 was pressed into temporary service, but its pilots were not familiar with Guam, or with the surrounding countryside.

The airport was also having its share of problems. The glide-slope (height-finding) element of the instrument landing system (ILS) had been withdrawn for upgrading about a month before the crash and the airfield's area surveillance radar was not working on the night in question. The weather was poor and visibility was limited.

Approaches to 06L were being flown on the ILS localiser only, with descent progress being monitored from a VOR/DME beacon some 3.3nm (6km) short of the touchdown point. The procedure in force at the time required the aircraft to be at 1,440ft as it passed over the beacon and then descend to a minimum safe altitude of 560ft as it passed the middle marker (which was less than a mile from touchdown). The runway itself was 256ft above mean sea level.

The Korean aircraft made a perfectly normal approach, but for some reason it was too low throughout and eventually hit Nimitz Hill — a 658ft high ridge on the extended centreline of the runway — some 3nm from the threshold. The cockpit voice recorder was recovered intact and its tape suggested that both pilots *thought* the VOR/DME beacon was located within the airfield boundary: in fact it was positioned on the summit of Nimitz Hill — which was exactly the reason for the safety-height requirement published in the temporary approach procedures.

The US NTSB report identified poor crew-coordination as the primary cause of the accident, but it went on to criticise KAL's crew-training regime and the lack of effective oversight of that regime by the Korean Civil Aviation Bureau. During the investigation it was discovered that the airfield controllers (following a number of false alerts) had disabled the aural alarm of their Minimum Safe Altitude Warning system: this did not shift responsibility from the flight crew, but its correct operation might have provided them with adequate warning of their position.

28 December 1997
United Airlines 747-100 N4723U

This aircraft was at cruise altitude over the Western Pacific — *en route* from Tokyo to Honolulu — when it ran into unusually severe clear-air turbulence, causing the death of one passenger and injuries to about 100 other people (both passengers and crew). The flight data recorder later revealed 1.8g positive and 0.8g negative accelerations, together with considerable airspeed fluctuations. The crew eventually regained control and made an uneventful landing.

5 March 1999
Air France 747-200F F-GPAN

As this cargo aircraft approached Meenambakam Airport at Chennai-Madras, India, the crew could not extend the nosegear, despite repeated efforts. During the subsequent forced-landing the nose was allowed to drop too early and the forward fuselage remained in contact with the runway surface for nearly 2,000m before the aircraft finally came to a halt.
The crew of five all escaped without serious injury but friction-induced sparks caused a major fire, which rapidly consumed the whole aircraft.

22 December 1999
Korean Airlines 747-285K HL7451

This JT9D-powered freighter had been airborne for little more than 55 seconds when it plunged into a wood some 1.5 miles (2.5km) south of the boundary of Stansted Airport, north of London. All four members of the crew lost their lives, but there were no casualties on the ground, although wreckage landed not far from some houses. The aircraft had just taken-off from runway 23 bound for Milan, in Italy, with a full load of assorted cargo on board. The wind was registered as 190°/18 knots; it was raining and the cloud base was estimated at 400-500ft (122–152m). Both flight recorders were eventually recovered in serviceable condition.

At the time of writing the investigation is still in progress, but early indications suggest that the captain's ADI (attitude director indicator — essentially the artificial horizon) had been *unreliable in roll* during the inbound flight. Some work had been done on the instrument during turnaround but the precise written record of this was lost in the post-impact explosion and fire. The cockpit voice recorder picked up sounds of the ADI-comparator audible alert system being triggered up to a dozen times, and the flight engineer was heard to be warning the captain about his excessive bank angle. The final report is yet to be issued.

8 PRODUCTION HISTORY

The details shown below represent all 747-100, 200, SP and 300 series aircraft manufactured at Everett between May 1969 and October 1991. They are listed in factory line-number order, because this is the only way of showing the chronological age of each airframe (Boeing construction numbers are allocated across the product range at the time of contract signature, and therefore bear little or no relationship to the actual order of construction). These are the original details of each aircraft when it was new: many of them have subsequently had a long history of ownership changes, conversions (to cargo or Combi configuration, for example) and periods of storage. A full service history of each airframe can be found in John Roach and Tony Eastwood's *Jet Airliner Production List,* published by The Aviation Hobby Shop, West Drayton, Middlesex.

Line No	Const'n No	Model No	First Operator	Delivery Reg	First Flight
1	20235	121	Boeing	N7470	9 Feb 69
2	19639	121	Pan Am	N747PA	11 Apr 69
3	19638	121	Pan Am	N732PA	10 Jul 69
4	19637	121	Pan Am	N731PA	10 May 69
5	19667	131	TWA	N93101	8 May 69
6	19640	121	Pan Am	N733PA	24 Oct 69
7	19641	121	Pan Am	N734PA	31 Oct 69
8	19668	131	TWA	N93102	7 Dec 69
9	19669	131	TWA	N93103	5 Dec 69
10	19642	121	Pan Am	N735PA	22 Dec 69
11	19643	121	Pan Am	N736PA	24 Dec 69
12	19746	130	Lufthansa	D-ABYA	18 Feb 70
13	19644	121	Pan Am	N737PA	9 Jan 70
14	19645	121	Pan Am	N738PA	19 Jan 70
15	19646	121	Pan Am	N739PA	25 Jan 70
16	19647	121	Pan Am	N740PA	31 Jan 70
17	19648	121	Pan Am	N741PA	13 Feb 70
18	19649	121	Pan Am	N742PA	18 Feb 70
19	19749	128	Air France	F-BPVA	28 Feb 70
20	19670	131	TWA	N93104	9 Feb 70
21	19671	131	TWA	N93105	23 Feb 70
22	19750	128	Air France	F-BPVB	7 Mar 70
23	19761	136	BOAC	G-AWNA	15 Mar 70
24	19650	121	Pan Am	N743PA	11 Mar 70
25	19651	121	Pan Am	N744PA	3 Mar 70
26	19652	121	Pan Am	N748PA	15 Mar 70
27	19778	151	Northwest Orient	N601US	7 Nov 70
28	19672	131	TWA	N93106	20 Mar 70
29	19747	130	Lufthansa	D-ABYB	30 Mar 70
30	19653	121	Pan Am	N749PA	21 Mar 70
31	19725	146	Japan AL	JA8101	31 Mar 70
32	19654	121	Pan Am	N750PA	1 Apr 70
33	19655	121	Pan Am	N751PA	6 Apr 70
34	19656	121	Pan Am	N752PA	10 Apr 70
35	19653	131	TWA	N93107	13 Apr 70
36	19729	143	Alitalia	I-DEMA	14 Apr 70
37	19657	121	Pan Am	N753PA	15 Apr 70
38	19674	131	TWA	N93108	19 Apr 70
39	19751	128	Air France	F-BPVC	26 Apr 70

Line No	Const'n No	Model No	First Operator	Delivery Reg	First Flight
40	19779	151	Northwest Orient	N602US	24 Apr 70
41	19762	136	BOAC	G-AWNB	6 May 70
42	19733	124	Continental AL	N26861	2 May 70
43	19675	131	TWA	N93109	13 May 70
44	19748	130	Lufthansa	D-ABYC	13 May 70
45	19780	151	Northwest Orient	N603US	10 May 70
46	20100	123	American AL	N9661	17 May 70
47	19658	121	Pan Am	N754PA	15 May 70
48	19763	136	BOAC	G-AWNC	28 May 70
49	19659	121	Pan Am	N755PA	21 May 70
50	19660	121	Pan Am	N770PA	21 May 70
51	19726	146	Japan AL	JA8102	16 May 70
52	19753	122	United AL	N4703U	6 Apr 70
53	19752	128	Air France	F-BPVD	6 Jun 70
54	19727	146	Japan AL	JA8103	9 Jun 70
55	19781	151	Northwest Orient	N604US	17 Jun 70
56	19730	143	Alitalia	I-DEME	13 Jun 70
57	20101	123	American AL	N9662	30 Jun 70
58	19734	124	Continental AL	N26862	2 Jul 70
59	20102	123	American AL	N9663	16 Jul 70
60	19754	122	United AL	N4704U	20 Jul 70
61	19755	122	United AL	N4710U	24 Jul 70
62	19782	151	Northwest Orient	N605US	11 Jul 70
63	19676	131	TWA	N53110	27 Jul 70

Cargolux 747-228F LX-DCV.

Line No	Const'n No	Model No	First Operator	Delivery Reg	First Flight
64	19735	124	Continental AL	N26863	17 Jul 70
65	20103	123	American AL	N9664	8 Jul 70
66	19756	122	United AL	N4711U	22 Jul 70
67	19757	122	United AL	N4712U	18 Aug 70
68	19918	135	National AL	N77772	21 Aug 70
69	20104	123	American AL	N9665	4 Sep 70
70	19661	121	Pan Am	N771PA	24 Jul 70
71	19783	151	Northwest Orient	N606US	22 Aug 70
72	19896	132	Delta AL	N9896	2 Sep 70
73	19677	131	TWA	N53111	15 Sep 70
74	19784	151	Northwest Orient	N607US	13 Aug 70
75	19785	151	Northwest Orient	N608US	4 Sep 70
76	19957	156	Iberia	EC-BRO	18 Sep 70
77	20105	123	American AL	N9666	22 Sep 70
78	19678	131	TWA	N53112	24 Sep 70
79	20106	123	American AL	N9667	24 Sep 70
80	20080	131	TWA	N93113	5 Oct 70
81	19919	135	National AL	N77773	7 Oct 70
82	19897	132	Delta AL	N9897	12 Oct 70
83	19786	151	Northwest Orient	N609US	29 Sep 70
84	19744	148	Aer Lingus	EI-ASI	3 Nov 70
85	20081	131	TWA	N93114	17 Oct 70
86	20107	123	American AL	N9668	15 Oct 70
87	20108	123	American AL	N9669	28 Oct 70
88	20356	251B	Northwest Orient	N611US	11 Oct 70
89	19875	122	United AL	N4713U	20 Oct 70
90	20109	123	American AL	N9670	1 Dec 70
91	19958	156	Iberia	EC-BRP	29 Oct 70
92	20401	129	Sabena	OO-SGA	3 Nov 70
93	19787	151	Northwest Orient	N610US	6 Nov 70
94	19898	132	Delta AL	N9898	6 Nov 70
95	20402	129	Sabena	OO-SGB	20 Nov 70
96	19922	206B	KLM	PH-BUA	13 Dec 70
97	19876	122	United AL	N4714U	13 Nov 70
98	20320	131	TWA	N93115	20 Dec 70
99	19877	122	United AL	N4716U	20 Nov 70
100	20207	127	Braniff AW	N601BN	9 Dec 70
101	19878	122	United AL	N4717U	7 Dec 70
102	20321	131	TWA	N53116	7 May 71
103	20347	121	Pan Am	N652PA	17 Dec 70
104	20013	133	Air Canada	CF-TOA	27 Jan 71
105	20355	128	Air France	F-BPVE	2 Feb 71
106	20348	121	Pan Am	N653PA	31 Dec 70
107	19764	136	BOAC	G-AWND	20 Jan 71
108	19745	148	Aer Lingus	EI-ASJ	4 Mar 71
109	19765	136	BOAC	G-AWNE	10 Feb 71
110	20349	121	Pan Am	N654PA	17 Apr 71
111	19766	136	BOAC	G-AWNF	16 Feb 71
112	20116	257B	Swissair	HB-IGA	15 Jan 71
113	20322	131	TWA	N93117	16 May 71
114	20120	283B	SAS	SE-DDL	26 Feb 71
115	20323	123	American AL	N9671	10 Feb 71
116	19823	246B	Japan AL	JA8104	29 Jan 71

Line No	Const'n No	Model No	First Operator	Delivery Reg	First Flight
117	20350	121	Pan Am	N655PA	3 May 71
118	19923	206B	KLM	PH-BUB	15 Feb 71
119	20324	123	American AL	N9672	17 Mar 71
120	19731	243B	Alitalia	I-DEMO	20 Feb 71
121	20014	133	Air Canada	CF-TOB	1 Mar 71
122	19824	246B	Japan AL	JA8105	12 Feb 71
123	20208	127	Wardair	CF-DJC	25 Mar 71
124	19959	237B	Air India	VT-EBD	8 Mar 71
125	20325	123	American AL	N9673	31 Mar 71
126	20117	257B	Swissair	HB-IGB	13 Mar 71
127	20351	121	Pan Am	N656PA	21 May 71
128	20493	230B	Lufthansa (Condor)	D-ABYF	17 Mar 71
129	20352	121	Pan Am	N657PA	27 May 71
130	19960	237B	Air India	VT-EBE	2 Apr 71
131	20353	121	Pan Am	N658PA	2 Jun 71
132	20372	230B	Lufthansa	D-ABYD	16 Apr 71
133	20326	123	American AL	N9674	23 Apr 71
134	19732	243B	Alitalia	I-DEMU	28 Apr 71
135	20357	251B	Northwest Orient	N612US	5 May 71
136	20390	123	American AL	N9675	7 May 71
137	19825	246B	Japan AL	JA8106	29 Apr 71
138	19924	206B	KLM	PH-BUC	9 May 71
139	19879	122	United AL	N4718U	16 May 71
140	20315	258B	El Al	4X-AXA	15 May 71
141	20358	251B	Northwest Orient	N613US	22 Jun 71
142	20354	121	Pan Am	N655PA	19 Jul 71
143	20391	123	American AL	N9676	11 Jun 71
144	20015	133	Air Canada	CF-TOC	11 Jun 71
145	19880	122	United AL	N4719U	16 May 71
146	20305	124	Continental AL	N26864	18 Jun 71
147	20009	238B	Qantas	VH-EBA	8 Jul 71
148	19881	122	United AL	N4720U	13 Jul 71
149	20010	238B	Qantas	VH-EBB	23 Jul 71
150	20269	136	BOAC	G-AWNG	30 Jul 71
151	20082	131	TWA	N93118	4 Aug 71
152	20398	206B	KLM	PH-BUD	6 Aug 71
153	20083	131	TWA	N93119	18 Aug 71
154	20237	244B	South African AW	ZS-SAL	28 Aug 71
155	20246	132	Delta AL	N9899	24 Aug 71
156	20399	206B	KLM	PH-BUE	3 Sep 71
157	20400	206B	KLM	PH-BUF	14 Sep 71
158	20238	244B	South African AW	ZS-SAM	5 Dec 71
159	20247	132	Delta AL	N9900	22 Sep 71
160	20239	244B	South African AW	ZS-SAN	30 Sep 71
161	20332	146	Japan AL	JA8107	4 Oct 71
162	20011	238B	Qantas	VH-EBC	7 Oct 71
163	20359	251B	Northwest Orient	N614US	13 Oct 71
164	20274	258B	El Al	4X-AXB	29 Oct 71
165	20360	251B	Northwest Orient	N615US	13 Nov 71
166	20333	246B	Japan AL	JA8108	25 Oct 71
167	20121	283B	SAS	OY-KHA	28 Oct 71
168	20373	230F	Lufthansa	D-ABYE	30 Nov 71
169	20270	136	BOAC	G-AWNH	9 Nov 71

Line No	Const'n No	Model No	First Operator	Delivery Reg	First Flight
170	20427	206B	KLM	PH-BUG	22 Nov 71
171	20012	238B	Qantas	VH-EBD	23 Nov 71
172	20271	136	BOAC	G-AWNI	3 Dec 71
173	20137	256B	Iberia	EC-BRQ	9 Dec 71
174	20376	128	Air France	F-BPVF	17 Jan 72
175	19882	122	United AL	N4723U	17 Dec 71
176	20377	128	Air France	F-BPVG	7 Jan 72
177	20378	128	Air France	F-BPVH	26 Jan 72
178	20501	282B	TAP	CS-TJA	4 Feb 72
179	20527	230B	Lufthansa	D-ABYG	9 Feb 72
180	20503	246B	Japan AL	JA8109	15 Feb 72
181	20504	246B	Japan AL	JA8110	24 Feb 72
182	20505	246B	Japan AL	JA8111	3 Mar 72
183	20272	136	BOAC	G-AWNJ	6 Mar 72
184	20273	136	BOAC	G-AWNK	10 Mar 72
185	20459	237B	Air India	VT-EBN	18 Mar 72
186	20559	230B	Lufthansa (Condor)	D-ABYH	17 Mar 72
187	20284	136	BOAC	G-AWNL	4 Apr 72
188	20558	237B	Air India	VT-EBO	14 Apr 72
189	20502	282B	TAP	CS-TJB	4 May 72
190	20520	243B	Alitalia	I-DEMB	11 May 72
191	20528	146	Japan AL	JA8112	26 May 72
192	20529	246B	Japan AL	JA8113	9 Jun 72
193	19883	122	United AL	N4727U	16 Jun 72
194	20556	244B	South African AW	ZS-SAO	14 Jul 72
195	20534	238B	Qantas	VH-EBE	27 Jul 72
196	20530	246B	Japan AL	JA8114	23 Aug 72
197	20531	146	Japan AL	JA8115	18 Aug 72
198	20557	244B	South African AW	ZS-SAP	15 Sep 72
199	20532	146	Japan AL	JA8116	6 Oct 72
200	20541	128	Air France	N28903	26 Oct 72
201	20542	128	Air France	N28888	30 Oct 72
202	20682	E-4A	US Air Force	31676	13 Jun 73
203	20543	128	Air France	N28899	11 Sep 72
204	20683	E-4A	US Air Force	31677	11 Sep 73
205	19925	122	United AL	N4728U	22 Jan 73
206	19926	122	United AL	N4729U	13 Jan 73
207	19927	122	United AL	N4732U	14 Feb 73
208	19928	122	United AL	N4735U	16 May 73
209	20651	273C	World AW	N747WA	23 Mar 73
210	20708	136	BOAC	G-AWNM	6 Apr 73
211	20652	273C	World AW	N748WA	25 Apr 73
212	20704	258B	El Al	4X-AXC	5 Apr 73
213	20770	2B5B	Korean AL	HL7410	16 Apr 73
214	20767	133	Air Canada	CF-TOD	3 May 73
215	20771	2B5B	Korean AL	HL7411	1 Jun 73
216	20742	284B	Olympic AW	SX-OAA	2 Jun 73
217	20535	238B	Qantas	VH-EBF	13 Jul 73
218	20712	212B	Singapore AL	9V-SIA	13 Jul 73
219	20713	212B	Singapore AL	9V-SIB	1 Aug 73
220	20809	136	BOAC/British AW	G-AWNN	20 Sep 73
221	20781	SR46	Japan AL	JA8117	31 Aug 73
222	20810	136	British AW	G-AWNO	18 Oct 73

Line No	Const'n No	Model No	First Operator	Delivery Reg	First Flight
223	20825	284B	Olympic AW	SX-OAB	12 Oct 73
224	20798	128	Air France	F-BPVL	25 Oct 73
225	20801	217B	CP Air	C-FCRA	2 Nov 73
226	20802	217B	CP Air	C-FCRB	15 Nov 73
227	20799	128	Air France	N63305	30 Nov 73
228	20800	128	Air France	N28366	10 Jan 74
229	20782	SR46	Japan AL	JA8118	10 Dec 73
230	20783	SR46	Japan AL	JA8119	28 Jan 74
231	20784	SR46	Japan AL	JA8120	8 Feb 74
232	20684	E-4A	US Air Force	40787	6 Jun 74
233	20841	238B	Qantas	VH-EBG	28 Feb 74
234	20923	SR46	Japan AL	JA8121	14 Mar 74
235	20924	246B	Japan AL	JA8122	21 Mar 74
236	20881	133	Air Canada	C-FTOE	19 Apr 74
237	20653	273C	World AW	N749WA	2 May 74
238	20842	238B	Qantas	VH-EBH	13 May 74
239	20928	282B	TAP	CS-TJC	30 May 74
240	20888	212B	Singapore AL	9V-SQC	21 Jun 74
241	20921	238B	Qantas	VH-EBI	28 Jun 74
242	20826	245F	Seaboard World	N701SW	12 Jul 74
243	21034	246F	Japan AL	JA8123	5 Aug 74
244	20927	217B	CP Air	C-FCRD	4 Oct 74
245	20887	228F	Air France	N18815	11 Sep 74
246	20952	136	British AW	G-AWNP	20 Sep 74
247	20929	217B	CP Air	C-FCRE	15 Nov 74
248	20953	136	British AW	G-BBPU	22 Oct 74
249	21032	SR46	Japan AL	JA8124	4 Nov 74
250	20977	233B Combi	Air Canada	C-GAGA	18 Nov 74
251	21030	246B	Japan AL	JA8125	4 Dec 74
252	20954	128	Air France	F-BPVP	18 Dec 74
253	21048	212B	Singapore AL	9V-SQD	20 Jan 75
254	21033	SR46	Japan AL	JA8126	24 Jan 75
255	21031	246B	Japan AL	JA8127	10 Feb 75
256	21035	282B	TAP	CS-TJD	22 Feb 75
257	20949	E-4B	US Air Force	50125	29 Apr 75
258	21120	251F	Northwest Orient	N616US	27 May 75
259	21029	146	Japan AL	JA8128	3 Apr 75
260	21054	238B	Qantas	VH-EBJ	21 Apr 75
261	21121	251F	Northwest Orient	N617US	23 Jun 75
262	21097	2B4B Combi	Middle East AL	OD-AGH	16 May 75
263	21098	2B4B Combi	Middle East AL	OD-AGI	5 Jun 75
264	21099	2B4B Combi	Middle East AL	OD-AGJ	7 Aug 75
265	21022	SP21	Pan Am	N530PA	4 Jul 75
266	20827	245F	Seaboard World	N702SW	7 Aug 75
267	21140	238B	Qantas	VH-EBK	15 Aug 75
268	21023	SP21	Pan Am	N531PA	14 Aug 75
269	21122	251F	Northwest Orient	N618US	15 Aug 75
270	21024	SP21	Pan Am	N532PA	10 Oct 75
271	21110	206B Combi	KLM	PH-BUH	26 Sep 75
272	21190	258C	El Al	4X-AXD	22 Oct 75
273	21025	SP21	Pan Am	N533PA	3 Nov 75
274	21189	287B	Aerolineas Argentinas	LV-LZD	11 Nov 75
275	20998	SP86	Iran Air	EP-IAA	20 Feb 76

Line No	Const'n No	Model No	First Operator	Delivery Reg	First Flight
276	21111	206B Combi	KLM	PH-BUI	26 Nov 75
277	21182	237B	Air India	VT-EDU	15 Dec 75
278	20999	SP86	Iran Air	EP-IAB	22 Apr 76
279	21141	128	Air France	N40116	27 Jan 76
280	21132	SP44	South African AW	ZS-SPA	17 Feb 76
281	21213	136	British AW	G-BDPV	25 Feb 76
282	21133	SP44	South African AW	ZS-SPB	10 Mar 76
283	21162	212B	Singapore AL	9V-SQE	19 Mar 76
284	21174	SP94	Syrianair	YK-AHA	15 Apr 76
285	21237	238B	Qantas	VH-EBL	14 Jun 76
286	21026	SP21	Pan Am	N534PA	7 May 76
287	21180	270C	Iraqi AW	YI-AGN	27 May 76
288	21134	SP44	South African AW	ZS-SPC	4 Jun 76
289	21181	270C	Iraqi AW	YI-AGO	21 Jun 76
290	21175	SP94	Syrianair	YK-AHB	1 Jul 76
291	21217	286B Combi	Iran Air	EP-IAG	21 Jul 76
292	21238	236B	British AW	G-BDXA	3 Sep 76
293	21253	SP44	South African AW	ZS-SPD	27 Aug 76
294	21220	230B Combi	Lufthansa	D-ABYJ	24 Sep 76
295	21255	228F	Air France	F-BPVR	28 Sep 76
296	21251	2D3B Combi	Alia	JY-AFA	12 Oct 76
297	21252	2D3B Combi	Alia	JY-AFB	26 Oct 76
298	21254	SP44	South African AW	ZS-SPE	5 Nov 76
299	21221	230B Combi	Lufthansa	D-ABYK	2 Dec 76
300	21218	286B Combi	Iran Air	EP-IAH	22 Dec 76
301	21263	SP44	South African AW	ZS-SPF	14 Jan 77
302	21239	236B	British AW	G-BDXB	22 Feb 77
303	21326	228B Combi	Air France	F-BPVS	4 Mar 77
304	21300	SP09	China AL	B-1862	18 Mar 77
305	21240	236B	British AW	G-BDXC	8 Apr 77
306	21441	SP21	Pan Am	N536PA	25 Apr 77
307	21093	SP86	Iran Air	EP-IAC	16 Mar 77
308	21321	251F	Northwest Orient	N616US	3 Jun 77
309	21316	212B	Singapore AL	9V-SQF	19 Jun 77
310	21352	238B	Qantas	VH-EBM	11 Jul 77
311	21381	283B Combi	SAS	LN-RNA	24 Aug 77
312	21439	212B	Singapore AL	9V-SQG	31 Aug 77
313	21429	228B Combi	Air France	F-BPVT	21 Sep 77
314	21354	238B Combi	Qantas	VH-ECA	4 Oct 77
315	21486	2J9F	Imperial Iranian AF	5-8113	28 Nov 77
316	21353	238B	Qantas	VH-EBN	6 Dec 77
317	21241	236B	British AW	G-BDXD	9 Jan 78
318	21446	237B	Air India	VT-EFJ	26 Jan 78
319	21487	2J9F	Imperial Iranian AF	5-8114	16 Feb 78
320	21380	230B Combi	Lufthansa	D-ABYL	2 Mar 78
321	21350	236B	British AW	G-BDXE	14 Mar 78
322	21454	209B Combi	China AL	B-1864	29 Mar 78
323	21351	236B	British AW	G-BDXF	10 Apr 78
324	21468	2Q2B Combi	Air Gabon	F-ODJG	25 Apr 78
325	21547	SP21	Pan Am	N537PA	5 May 78
326	21516	211B	Wardair	C-GXRA	15 May 78
327	21594	258C	El Al	4X-AXF	7 Jun 78
328	21536	236B	British AW	G-BDXG	2 Jun 78

Line No	Const'n No	Model No	First Operator	Delivery Reg	First Flight
329	21652	SP68	Saudi Government	HZ-NM1	28 Aug 78
330	21473	237B	Air India	VT-EFO	19 Jun 78
331	21548	SP21	Pan Am	N538PA	30 Jun 78
332	21541	269B Combi	Kuwait AW	9K-ADA	17 Jul 78
333	21537	228B Combi	Air France	N1252E	21 Jul 78
334	21576	228F	Air France	F-BPVV	27 Jul 78
335	21542	269B Combi	Kuwait AW	9K-ADB	3 Aug 78
336	21549	206B Combi	KLM	PH-BUK	17 Aug 78
337	21515	2B3F	UTA	F-GPAN	21 Aug 78
338	21615	2B6B Combi	Royal Air Maroc	CN-RME	6 Sep 78
339	21657	238B	Qantas	VH-EBO	8 Sep 78
340	21507	2J9F	Imperial Iranian AF	5-8115	18 Sep 78
341	21658	238B	Qantas	VH-EBP	21 Sep 78
342	21588	230B Combi	Lufthansa	D-ABYM	2 Oct 78
343	21514	2J9F	Imperial Iranian AF	5-8116	11 Oct 78
344	21550	206B Combi	KLM	PH-BUL	17 Oct 78
345	21589	230B	Lufthansa	D-ABYN	25 Oct 78
346	21604	SR81	All Nippon	JA8133	3 Nov 78
347	21592	230F	Lufthansa	D-ABYO	10 Nov 78
348	21590	230B	Lufthansa	D-ABYP	22 Nov 78
349	21725	287B	Aerolineas Argentinas	LV-MLO	8 Dec 78
350	21591	230B	Lufthansa	D-ABYQ	1 Dec 78
351	21605	SR81	All Nippon	JA8134	9 Dec 78
352	21643	230B Combi	Lufthansa	D-ABYR	16 Dec 78
353	21614	2B2B Combi	Air Madagascar	5R-MFT	12 Jan 79
354	21650	2R7F	Cargolux	LX-DCV	23 Jan 79
355	21627	233B Combi	Air Canada	C-GAGB	16 Jan 79
356	21644	230B Combi	Lufthansa	D-ABYS	23 Jan 79
357	21704	251B	Northwest Orient	N622US	15 Feb 79
358	21575	283B Combi	SAS	SE-DFZ	17 Feb 79
359	21543	269B Combi	Kuwait AW	9K-ADC	14 Feb 79
360	21606	SR81	All Nippon	JA8135	21 Feb 79
361	21678	246B	Japan AL	JA8129	24 Feb 79
362	21737	258F	El Al	4X-AXG	7 Mar 79
363	21772	2B5B	Korean AL	HL7443	8 Mar 79
364	21731	228B Combi	Air France	F-BPVX	15 Mar 79
365	21635	236B	British AW	G-BDXH	19 Mar 79
366	21773	2B5B	Korean AL	HL7445	23 Mar 79
367	21648	SP21	Pan Am	N539PA	30 Mar 79
368	21517	211B	Wardair	C-GXRD	2 Apr 79
369	21659	206B Combi	KLM	PH-BUM	9 Apr 79
370	21745	228B	Air France	F-BPVY	13 Apr 79
371	21758	SP86	Iran Air	EP-IAD	26 Apr 79
372	21730	259B Combi	Avianca	HK-2300	11 May 79
373	21649	SP21	Pan Am	N540PA	1 May 79
374	21705	251B	Northwest Orient	N623US	11 May 79
375	21682	227B	Braniff AW	N602BN	17 May 79
376	21679	246B	Japan AL	JA8130	31 May 79
377	21706	251B	Northwest Orient	N624US	26 May 79
378	21707	251B	Northwest Orient	N625US	8 Jun 79
379	21708	251B	Northwest Orient	N626US	21 Jun 79
380	21680	246B	Japan AL	JA8131	20 Jun 79
381	21759	186B	Iran Air	EP-IAM	20 Jun 79

British Airways 747F, the aptly numbered G-KILO.

Line No	Const'n No	Model No	First Operator	Delivery Reg	First Flight
382	21681	246F	Japan AL	JA8132	27 Jun 79
383	21825	240B Combi	Pakistan Int AL	AP-BAK	2 Jul 79
384	21743	221F	Pam Am	N904PA	5 Jul 79
385	21746	267B	Cathay Pacific	VR-HKG	9 Jul 79
386	21843	209B	China AL	B-1866	16 Jul 79
387	21683	212B	Singapore AL	9V-SQH	2 Aug 79
388	21835	2B3F	UTA	F-GBOX	25 Jul 79
389	21660	206B Combi	KLM	PH-BUN	3 Aug 79
390	21829	237B	Air India	VT-EFU	3 Aug 79
391	21684	212B	Singapore AL	9V-SQI	9 Aug 79
392	21744	221F	Pan Am	N905PA	11 Aug 79
393	21922	SR81	All Nippon	JA8136	21 Aug 79
394	21764	245F	Seaboard World	N703SW	25 Aug 79
395	21923	SR81	All Nippon	JA8137	25 Aug 79
396	21841	245F	Seaboard World	N704SW	16 Sep 79
397	21848	206B	KLM	PH-BUO	6 Sep 79
398	21787	228F	Air France	F-BPVZ	7 Sep 79
399	21935	212B	Singapore AL	9V-SQJ	17 Sep 79
400	21668	2J9F	Imperial Iranian AF	5-8117	17 Sep 79
401	21936	212B	Singapore AL	9V-SQK	25 Sep 79
402	21782	2D7B	Thai AW Int	HS-TGA	1 Oct 79
403	21726	287B	Aerolineas Argentinas	LV-MLP	1 Oct 79
404	21727	287B	Aerolineas Argentinas	LV-MLR	5 Oct 79
405	21785	SP27	Braniff AW	N603BN	7 Oct 79

Line No	Const'n No	Model No	First Operator	Delivery Reg	First Flight
406	21827	249F	Flying Tiger	N806FT	15 Oct 79
407	22064	246B	Japan AL	JA8140	18 Oct 79
408	21828	249F	Flying Tiger	N807FT	1 Nov 79
409	21977	238B Combi	Qantas	VH-ECB	25 Oct 79
410	22145	238B	Qantas	VH-EBQ	28 Nov 79
411	22065	246B	Japan AL	JA8141	12 Nov 79
412	21709	251B	Northwest Orient	N627US	21 Dec 79
413	21786	SP27	Braniff AW	N614BN	29 Nov 79
414	21993	237B	Air India	VT-EGA	11 Dec 79
415	21961	SP31	TWA	N58201	2 Dec 79
416	21964	271C	Transamerica AL	N741TV	30 Nov 79
417	21783	2D7B	Thai AW Int	HS-TGB	3 Dec 79
418	22254	258B	El Al	4X-AXH	6 Dec 79
419	21937	212B	Singapore AL	9V-SQL	14 Jan 80
420	21924	SR81	All Nippon	JA8138	18 Dec 79
421	21832	2F6B	Philippine AL	N741PR	14 Dec 79
422	21925	SR81	All Nippon	JA8139	15 Jan 80
423	21833	2F6B	Philippine AL	N742PR	7 Jan 80
424	21784	2D7B	Thai AW Int	HS-TGC	4 Feb 80
425	21834	2F6B	Philippine AL	N743PR	17 Jan 80
426	22066	SR46	Japan AL	JA8142	21 Jan 80
427	22067	SR46	Japan AL	JA8143	25 Jan 80
428	21982	228B	Air France	F-GCBA	30 Jan 80
429	22077	240B Combi	Pakistan Int AW	AP-BAT	2 Feb 80
430	21830	236B	British AW	G-BDXI	16 Feb 80
431	21994	237B	Air India	VT-EGB	7 Feb 80
432	22063	246F	Japan AL	JA8144	24 Feb 80
433	21932	SPJ6	CAAC	B-2442	14 Feb 80
434	21995	237B	Air India	VT-EGC	28 Feb 80
435	22105	2L5B Combi	Varig	PP-VNA	28 Feb 80
436	21938	212B	Singapore AL	9V-SQM	10 Mar 80
437	21991	227B	Northwest Orient	N633US	25 Mar 80
438	21965	271C	Transamerica AL	N742TV	8 Mar 80
439	21962	SP31	TWA	N58202	12 Mar 80
440	21831	236B	British AW	G-BDXJ	26 Mar 80
441	21963	SP31	TWA	N57203	11 Apr 80
442	22389	251F	Northwest Orient	N628US	21 Mar 80
443	22106	2L5B Combi	Varig	PP-VNB	26 Mar 80
444	22388	251F	Northwest Orient	N629US	1 Apr 80
445	22298	SP09	China AL	B-1880	18 Apr 80
446	21966	267B	Cathay Pacific	VR-HIA	7 Apr 80
447	21992	SP27	Braniff AW	N606BN	19 May 80
448	22480	2B5F	Korean AL	HL7451	30 Apr 80
449	21939	212B	Singapore AL	9V-SQN	13 May 80
450	22238	256B	Iberia	EC-DIA	23 Apr 80
451	22239	256B	Iberia	EC-DIB	2 May 80
452	22246	2U3B	Garuda	PK-GSA	12 Jun 80
453	22291	SR81	All Nippon	JA8145	3 May 80
454	22481	2B5F	Korean AL	HL7452	4 Jun 80
455	21933	SPJ6	CAAC	B-2444	6 Jun 80
456	22292	SR81	All Nippon	JA8146	23 May 80
457	21940	212B	Singapore AL	9V-SQO	12 Jun 80
458	22245	249F	Flying Tiger	N808FT	20 Jun 80

Line No	Const'n No	Model No	First Operator	Delivery Reg	First Flight
459	22247	2U3B	Garuda	PK-GSB	3 Jul 80
460	22237	249F	Flying Tiger	N810FT	31 Jul 80
461	22248	2U3B	Garuda	PK-GSC	22 Jul 80
462	22272	228B Combi	Air France	N1289E	18 Jun 80
463	22299	209F	China AL	B-1894	11 Jul 80
464	22614	238B	Qantas	VH-EBR	24 Jun 80
465	22234	227B	Northwest Orient	N634US	14 Jan 81
466	22149	267B	Cathay Pacific	VR-HIB	30 Jun 80
467	21934	SPJ6	CAAC	N1304E	11 Jul 80
468	22249	2U3B	Garuda	PK-GSD	8 Aug 80
469	22107	2L5B	Varig	PP-VNC	5 Dec 80
470	21941	212B	Singapore AL	9V-SQP	15 Aug 80
471	21942	212B	Singapore AL	9V-SQQ	11 Sep 80
472	22169	2S4F	Air Afrique	TU-TAP	12 Sep 80
473	22302	SP27	CAAC	N1301E	2 Dec 80
474	22376	206B Combi	KLM	N1295E	6 Aug 80
475	21943	212B	Singapore AL	9V-SQR	16 Oct 80
476	22150	245F	Flying Tiger	N815FT	22 Sep 80
477	22293	SR81	All Nippon	JA8147	15 Aug 80
478	22151	245F	Flying Tiger	N816FT	3 Oct 80
479	22337	2D7B	Thai AW Int	HS-TGF	11 Sep 80
480	22306	236F	British AW	G-KILO	19 Sep 80
481	22294	SR81	All Nippon	JA8148	30 Sep 80
482	22390	2R7F	Cargolux	LX-ECV	30 Sep 80
483	22615	238B Combi	Qantas	VH-ECC	29 Sep 80
484	22482	2B5B	Korean AL	HL7454	17 Oct 80
485	22427	228B Combi	Air France	F-GCBC	7 Oct 80
486	22170	244B Combi	South African AW	ZS-SAR	24 Nov 80
487	22297	287B	Aerolineas Argentinas	LV-OEP	4 Nov 80
488	22171	244B Combi	South African AW	ZS-SAS	12 Oct 80
489	22478	246B	Japan AL	JA8149	26 Nov 80
490	22363	230B	Lufthansa	D-ABYT	4 Nov 80
491	22379	206B Combi	KLM	N1298E	6 Nov 80
492	22506	243B Combi	Alitalia	I-DEMC	14 Nov 80
493	22429	267B	Cathay Pacific	VR-HIC	5 Dec 80
494	22477	246F	Japan AL	JA8151	26 Nov 80
495	22303	236B	British AW	G-BDXK	16 Jan 81
496	22479	246B	Japan AL	JA8150	13 Dec 80
497	22507	243B Combi	Alitalia	I-DEMD	26 Nov 80
498	22382	2F6B	Philippine AL	N744PR	2 Dec 80
499	22508	243B Combi	Alitalia	I-DEMF	11 Dec 80
500	22381	283B Combi	SAS	N4501Q	20 Dec 80
501	22483	SPB5	Korean AL	HL7456	23 Dec 80
502	22304	236B	Malaysian AL	9M-MHI	24 Jan 81
503	22428	228B Combi	Air France	N1305E	23 Dec 80
504	22471	2D7B	Thai AW Int	HS-TGG	16 Jan 81
505	22495	SP38	Qantas	VH-EAA	11 Jan 81
506	22305	236B	British AW	G-BDXL	12 Feb 81
507	22484	SPB5	Korean AL	HL7457	30 Jan 81
508	22378	2H7B Combi	Cameroon AL	TJ-CAB	6 Feb 81
509	22454	256B	Iberia	EC-DLC	16 Feb 81
510	21944	212B	Singapore AL	9V-SQS	18 Feb 81
511	22594	SR81	All Nippon	JA8152	18 Feb 81

Line No	Const'n No	Model No	First Operator	Delivery Reg	First Flight
512	22498	168B	Saudia	HZ-AIA	2 Mar 81
513	22485	2B5B	Korean AL	HL7458	6 Mar 81
514	22579	2D3B	Alia	JY-AFS	9 Mar 81
515	22455	256B	Iberia	EC-DID	12 Mar 81
516	22595	SR81	All Nippon	JA8153	29 Mar 81
517	22499	168B	Saudia	HZ-AIB	23 Mar 81
518	22514	2B3B Combi	UTA	F-BTDG	1 Apr 81
519	22446	209B	China AL	B-1886	7 Apr 81
520	22486	2B5F	Korean AL	HL7459	10 Apr 81
521	22515	2B3B Combi	UTA	F-BTDH	17 Apr 81
522	22500	168B	Saudia	HZ-AIC	23 Apr 81
523	22722	219B	Air New Zealand	ZK-NZV	6 May 81
524	22403	271C	Transamerica	N743TV	1 May 81
525	22501	168B	Saudia	HZ-AID	8 May 81
526	22442	236B	Malaysian AL	9M-MHJ	21 May 81
527	22723	219B	Air New Zealand	ZK-NZW	22 May 81
528	22724	219B	Air New Zealand	ZK-NZX	12 Feb 81
529	22503	SP68	Saudia	HZ-AIF	4 Jun 81
530	22502	168B	Saudia	HZ-AIE	11 Jun 81
531	22530	267B	Cathay Pacific	VR-HID	15 Jun 81
532	22592	287B	Aerolineas Argentinas	LV-OOZ	24 Jun 81
533	22510	243B	Alitalia	I-DEMG	1 Jul 81
534	22547	SP09	China AL	N4508H	20 Jul 81
535	22678	228F	Air France	N4508E	20 Jul 81
536	22511	243B	Alitalia	I-DEML	28 Jul 81
537	22672	SP38	Qantas	VH-EAB	3 Aug 81
538	22668	230F	Lufthansa	D-ABYU	13 Aug 81
539	22380	206B Combi	KLM	N1309E	21 Aug 81
540	22496	283B Combi	SAS	N4502R	26 Aug 81
541	22709	SR81	All Nippon	JA8156	21 Sep 81
542	22512	243B	Alitalia	I-DEMN	21 Sep 81
543	22616	238B	Qantas	VH-EBS	25 Sep 81
544	22710	SR81	All Nippon	JA8157	15 Oct 81
545	22545	243F	Alitalia	I-DEMR	15 Oct 81
546	22513	243B	Alitalia	I-DEMP	2 Nov 81
547	22745	246B	Japan AL	JA8154	4 Nov 81
548	22746	246B	Japan AL	JA8155	17 Nov 81
549	22669	230B Combi	Lufthansa	D-ABYW	19 Nov 81
550	22670	230B Combi	Lufthansa	D-ABYX	1 Dec 81
551	22747	168B	Saudia	HZ-AIG	11 Dec 81
552	22593	287B	Aerolineas Argentinas	LV-OPA	16 Dec 81
553	22740	269B Combi	Kuwait AW	9K-ADD	14 Jan 82
554	22764	256B	Iberia	EC-DNP	25 Jan 82
555	22748	168B	Saudia	HZ-AIH	13 Feb 82
556	22447	209B	China AL	B-1888	17 Feb 82
557	22749	168B	Saudia	HZ-AII	19 Mar 82
558	22794	228B	Air France	N4506H	17 Mar 82
559	22711	SR81	All Nippon	JA8158	1 Apr 82
560	22750	SP68	Saudia	HZ-AIJ	13 Apr 82
561	22768	2U3B	Garuda	PK-GSE	24 Apr 82
562	22769	2U3B	Garuda	PK-GSF	8 May 82
563	22725	219B	Air New Zealand	ZK-NZY	27 May 82
564	22805	SP09	China AL	N4522V	10 Jun 82

Line No	Const'n No	Model No	First Operator	Delivery Reg	First Flight
565	22366	270C	Iraqi AW	YI-AGP	25 Jun 82
566	22872	267B	Cathay Pacific	VR-HIE	9 Jul 82
567	22858	SP70	Iraqi Government	YI-ALM	2 Aug 82
568	22791	219B	Air New Zealand	ZK-NZZ	5 Aug 82
569	22939	228F	Air France	N4544F	25 Aug 82
570	22704	357 Combi	Swissair	HB-IGC	5 Oct 82
571	22989	246F	Japan AL	N211JL	7 Oct 82
572	22712	SR81	All Nippon	JA8159	23 Oct 82
573	22870	3B3	UTA	F-GDUA	10 Dec 82
574	22672	230B Combi	Lufthansa	D-ABYY	4 Dec 82
575	22969	243B	Alitalia	I-DEMS	11 Feb 83
576	22705	357 Combi	Swissair	HB-IGD	14 Feb 83
577	22970	344	South African AW	ZS-SAT	16 Feb 83
578	22971	344	South African AW	ZS-SAU	27 Mar 83
579	22990	246B	Japan AL	JA8161	25 Apr 83
580	23026	312	Singapore AL	9V-SKA	15 Apr 83
581	22991	246B	Japan AL	JA8162	17 May 83
582	23048	267B	Cathay Pacific	VR-HIF	13 May 83
583	23027	312	Singapore AL	N116KB	12 Jun 83
584	23028	312	Singapore AL	N117KC	23 Jun 83
585	22995	357	Swissair	N221GE	22 Sep 83
586	22996	357	Swissair	N221GF	12 Sep 83
587	23056	306 Combi	KLM	N4548M	15 Sep 83
588	23067	346	Japan AL	N212JL	10 Oct 83
589	23068	346	Japan AL	N213JL	26 Oct 83
590	23029	312	Singapore AL	N118KD	11 Nov 83
591	23071	2J6B	CAAC	B-2446	6 Dec 83
592	23070	3G1	Saudi Government	HZ-HM1A	15 Dec 83
593	23030	312	Singapore AL	N119KE	1 Feb 84
594	23111	251B	Northwest Orient	N631US	28 Feb 84
595	23112	251B	Northwest Orient	N632US	27 Mar 84
596	23120	267B	Cathay Pacific	VR-HIH	17 Apr 84
597	22472	2D7B	Thai AW Int	HS-TGS	16 May 84
598	23031	312	Singapore AL	N120KF	18 Jun 84
599	23149	346	Japan AL	JA8163	7 Nov 84
600	23137	306	KLM	N4551N	9 Aug 84
601	23150	146B	Japan AL	JA8164	25 Oct 84
602	23222	338	Qantas	VH-EBT	6 Oct 84
603	23032	312	Singapore AL	N121KG	17 Oct 84
604	23138	281F	Nippon Air Cargo	JA8167	19 Nov 84
605	22487	3B5B	Korean AL	HL7468	3 Dec 84
606	23223	338	Qantas	VH-EBU	21 Dec 84
607	23151	346	Japan AL	JA8166	17 Jan 85
608	23139	281F	Nippon Air Cargo	JA8168	20 Feb 85
609	23033	312	Singapore AL	N122KH	1 Mar 85
610	23224	338	Qantas	VH-EBV	21 Mar 85
611	22489	3B5B	Korean AL	HL7469	30 Mar 85
612	23243	312B	Singapore AL	N123KJ	19 Apr 85
613	23300	243B Combi	Alitalia	I-DEMT	8 May 85
614	23286	230B Combi	Lufthansa	D-ABYZ	16 May 85
615	23221	367	Cathay Pacific	VR-HII	31 May 85
616	23262	368	Saudia	HZ-AIK	13 Jun 85
617	23287	230B Combi	Lufthansa	D-ABZA	21 Jun 85

Line No	Const'n No	Model No	First Operator	Delivery Reg	First Flight
618	23301	243B	Alitalia	I-DEMV	12 Jul 85
619	23263	368	Saudia	HZ-AIL	26 Jul 85
620	23264	368	Saudia	HZ-AIM	6 Aug 85
621	23244	312B	Singapore AL	N124KK	23 Aug 85
622	23265	368	Saudia	HZ-AIN	10 Oct 85
623	23350	281F	Nippon Air Cargo	JA8172	1 Oct 85
624	23266	368	Saudia	HZ-AIO	9 Oct 85
625	23348	230F	Lufthansa	D-ABZB	15 Oct 85
626	23245	312B	Singapore AL	N125KL	5 Nov 85
627	23394	341 Combi	Varig	PP-VNH	12 Nov 85
628	23461	2J6B	CAAC	B-2448	30 Nov 85
629	23395	341 Combi	Varig	PP-VNI	13 Dec 85
630	23267	368	Saudia	HZ-AIP	3 Jan 86
631	23268	368	Saudia	HZ-AIQ	14 Jan 86
632	23413	3B3	UTA	F-GETA	23 Jan 86
633	23393	230B	Lufthansa	D-ABZC	24 Jan 86
634	23392	367	Cathay Pacific	VR-HIJ	8 Feb 86
635	23389	246B	Japan AL	JA8169	1 Mar 86
636	23390	346SR	Japan AL	JA8170	26 Feb 86
637	23409	312 Combi	Singapore AL	9V-SKM	10 Mar 86
638	23408	338	Qantas	VH-EBW	19 Mar 86
639	23407	230B	Lufthansa	D-ABZD	31 Mar 86
640	23482	346	Japan AL	JA8173	6 Apr 86
641	23480	3B3	UTA	F-GETB	14 Apr 86
642	23547	251B	Northwest Orient	N636US	22 Apr 86
643	23269	368	Saudia	HZ-AIR	1 May 86
644	23548	251B	Northwest Orient	N637US	10 May 86
645	23270	368	Saudia	HZ-AIS	19 May 86
646	23439	329	Sabena	OO-SGC	29 May 86
647	23476	243B	Alitalia	I-DEMW	6 Jun 86
648	23501	281B	All Nippon	JA8174	16 Jun 86
649	23502	281B	All Nippon	JA8175	23 Jun 86
650	23600	3H6 Combi	Malaysian AL	9M-MHK	2 Jul 86
651	23549	251B	Northwest Orient	N638US	11 Jul 86
652	23271	368	Saudia	HZ-AIT	23 Jul 86
653	23410	312 Combi	Singapore AL	9V-SKN	12 Aug 86
654	23391	246F	Japan AL	JA8171	19 Aug 86
655	23637	346SR	Japan AL	JA8176	29 Aug 86
656	23611	228B	Air France	F-GCBH	8 Sep 86
657	23508	306	KLM	PH-BUW	20 Sep 86
658	23638	346	Japan AL	JA8177	22 Sep 86
659	23534	367	Cathay Pacific	VR-HIK	3 Oct 86
660	23621	230F	Lufthansa	D-ABZF	14 Oct 86
661	23676	228B Combi	Air France	F-GCBI	10 Oct 86
662	23688	338	Qantas	VH-EBX	26 Oct 86
663	23509	230B Combi	Lufthansa	D-ABZE	16 Nov 86
664	23639	346	Japan AL	JA8178	3 Dec 86
665	23622	230B	Lufthansa	D-ABZH	17 Dec 86
666	23769	312 Combi	Singapore AL	9V-SKP	16 Jan 87
667	23698	281B	All Nippon	JA8181	13 Dec 86
668	23640	346	Japan AL	JA8179	25 Jan 87
669	23652	21AC	Martinair	PH-MCE	5 Feb 87
670	23746	2J6B	CAAC	B-2450	20 Feb 87

Line No	Const'n No	Model No	First Operator	Delivery Reg	First Flight
671	23709	367	Cathay Pacific	VR-HOL	1 Feb 87
672	23711	236B Combi	British AW	G-BDXM	13 Feb 87
673	23736	222B	United AL	N151UA	1 Mar 87
674	23735	236B Combi	British AW	G-BDXN	10 Mar 87
675	23737	222B	United AL	N152UA	16 Mar 87
676	23610	SPZ5	UAE Government	A6-ZSN	31 Mar 87
677	23799	236B	British AW	G-BDXO	10 Apr 87
678	23823	338	Qantas	VH-EBY	18 Apr 87
679	23824	VC-25A	US Air Force	82-8000	16 May 87
680	23887	251F	Northwest AL	N638US	18 May 87
681	23721	3D7	Thai AW Int	HS-TGD	22 Jun 87
682	23888	251F	Northwest AL	N640US	18 Jun 87
683	23813	281B	All Nippon	JA8182	30 Jun 87
684	23641	246F	Japan AL	JA8180	29 Jul 87
685	23825	VC-25A	US Air Force	92-9000	29 Oct 87
686	23751	357 Combi	Swissair	HB-IGG	26 Aug 87
687	23864	267F	Cathay Pacific	VR-HVZ	11 Sep 87
688	23722	3D7	Thai AW Int	HS-TGE	16 Nov 87
689	23919	281F	Nippon Cargo AL	JA8188	21 Dec 87
690	23920	367	Cathay Pacific	VR-HOM	23 Oct 87
691	23969	346	Japan AL	JA8185	15 Feb 88
692	23967	346SR	Japan AL	JA8183	24 Nov 87
693	23968	346SR	Japan AL	JA8184	22 Dec 87
694	24018	346SR	Japan AL	JA8186	21 Jan 88
695	24019	346SR	Japan AL	JA8187	21 Jan 88
696	23719	451*	Northwest AL	N661US	29 Apr 88

*Line No 696 was the first of the 400-series aircraft, which ultimately led to the end of Classic 747 production. Gaps in the following line-number sequence represent an increasing number of production slots being allocated to the updated, digital-cockpit model.

697	24088	236B	British AW	G-BDXO	13 Feb 88
698	24067	228B	Air France	F-GCBJ	2 Mar 88
699	24071	256B	Iberia	EC-EEK	25 Mar 88
701	24106	341	Varig	PP-VOA	24 Apr 88
702	24107	341	Varig	PP-VOB	7 May 88
703	24108	341	Varig	PP-VOC	18 May 88
704	24161	366 Combi	Egyptair	SU-GAL	7 Jun 88
706	24138	230F	Lufthansa	D-ABZI	19 Jun 88
707	24162	366 Combi	Egyptair	SU-GAM	25 Jun 88
709	24215	367	Cathay Pacific	VR-HON	12 Jul 88
710	24177	212F	Singapore AL	9V-SKQ	11 Aug 88
711	24159	337	Air India	VT-EPW	26 Sep 88
712	24134	21AC	Martinair	PH-MCF	15 Sep 88
713	24194	3B5	Korean Air	HL7470	21 Aug 88
714	24158	228F	Air France	F-GCBK	11 Sep 88
716	24156	346	Japan Asia AW	JA8189	4 Oct 88
718	24195	2B5F	Korean Air	HL7475	15 Oct 88
719	24160	337	Air India	VT-EPX	8 Nov 88
720	24196	2B5F	Korean Air	HL7476	16 Nov 88
724	24359	268F	Saudia	HZ-AIU	11 Dec 88
752	24308	209F	China AL	B-160	13 Aug 89
772	24735	228F	Air France	F-GCBL	9 Feb 90

Line No	Const'n No	Model No	First Operator	Delivery Reg	First Flight
776	24586	267F	Cathay Pacific	VR-HVX	22 Feb 90
810	24837	329	Sabena	OO-SGD	5 Sep 90
814	24960	2J6F	Air China	B-2462	26 Sep 90
818	24576	281F	Nippon Cargo AL	JA8191	16 Oct 90
822	24879	228F	Air France	F-GCBM	5 Nov 90
878	25266	228F	Air France	F-GCBN	19 Sep 91
886**	25171	281F	Nippon Cargo AL	JA8194	4 Nov 91

**Line No 886 was the last of the so-called Classic 747s. All subsequent airframes were manufactured with the two-crew, digital cockpit and extended wing of the 747-400.

Aerolineas Argentinas 747-287B LV-LZD.

9 CHRONOLOGY

Oct 62 DoD/USAF Operational Requirement CX-4 released to industry: specifies 18ft wide cargo deck.

Nov 63 Op. Req. CX-4 superseded by Op. Req. CX-X, which added very high by-pass turbofans to the requirement.

Early 64 Op. Req. CX-X superseded by Op. Req. CX-HLS (Cargo Experimental — Heavy Logistics System) — which finally gave life to the military programme.

May 64 CX-HLS competitive bids submitted to USAF Systems Command at Wright Field.

May 64 Boeing expresses interest in a programme to stretch the 707 airliner to a capacity of more than 200 passengers.

End 64 Boeing; Douglas; Lockheed; Pratt & Whitney and General Electric, all receive full *Project Definition* contracts for CX-HLS airframes and engines.

Feb 65 Boeing gives details of 'domestic' 707-620 and 'intercontinental' 707-820.

5 Apr 65 Douglas announces higher-capacity 60-series DC-8s and reveals launch orders from Eastern, SAS and United Airlines.

Aug 65 Lockheed wins the CX-HLS contract (with the aircraft which later became the C-5A Galaxy).

Oct 65 Boeing begins to talk to airlines about a proposed wide-body airliner, based in part on the earlier CX-HLS submission.

Jan 66 First details announced of a proposed twin-deck 747, based on a 'double-bubble' fuselage structure.

Apr 66 First details announced of a single-deck, production version of the 747: now optimised for eventual cargo operation.

13 Apr 66 Bill Allen, Chairman of Boeing, announces conditional launch of 747 programme, together with Pan Am's order for 25 aircraft.

Jun 66 Boeing leases a 780-acre green-field site at Everett, Wash, to build new factory for final assembly of 747s.

25 Jul 66 Formal go-ahead of 747 programme cancels all escape clauses in supplier/customer contracts: Boeing now fully committed.

Mar 68 Boeing announces a proposed tri-jet version of the 747 with a fin-mounted JT9D: project dropped just 6 weeks later.

Apr 68 Tri-jet 747 dropped in favour of a proposed twin-engined version using a smaller body and wing.

Jun 68 Pratt & Whitney JT9D engine flight tested for the first time, on starboard-inner pylon of leased B-52 bomber.

30 Sep 68 Roll-out of the first 747 from the purpose-built factory at Everett — just 30 months after the programme was launched.

Dec 68 Boeing announces the 747B, with more power, longer range and a max t/o weight of 775,000lb: later became 747-200.

9 Feb 69 First flight of the 747 'prototype' (N7470, piloted by Jack Waddell: flight cut short because of a leading-edge flap problem).

28 Feb 69 Roll-out of the second aircraft (N747PA) — which was ultimately destined to go into service with Pan Am.

11 Apr 69 First flight of the second aircraft (N747PA).

Jul 69 All five aircraft for the Test and Certification programme had flown by 10 July.

Jul 69 The fourth aircraft (N731PA) was demonstrated at the Paris Air Show.

Oct 69 Pan Am cancels its plans for a December launch of passenger services: major problems with the JT9D engine installation.

Dec 69 First deliveries to Pan Am (N733PA and N734PA), and to TWA (N93102), under restricted C of A for crew training only.

30 Dec 69 747 receives its full passenger-carrying Certificate of Airworthiness from the FAA.

12 Jan 70 First (unsuccessful) proving flight by Pan Am 747 into London Airport: planned European tour curtailed by engine problems.

22 Jan 70 First passenger-carrying flight left New York (6hr late due to engine problems), bound for London.

11 Oct 70 First flight of the uprated 747B — which later became known as the 747-200 series. (N611US, 747-251B for Northwest Orient).

23 Dec 70 FAA Certification granted to 747B — now known as the 747-200.

30 Nov 71 First flight of the 747-200F freighter version (D-ABYE, a 747-230F destined for Lufthansa).

7 Mar 72 FAA Certification granted to 747-200F.

30 Oct 72 Boeing announces 747SR (Short Range): new model for Japanese domestic market. JAL order for four also announced.

23 Mar 73 First flight of 747-200C Convertible passenger/cargo model. (N747WA, a 747-273C destined for World Airways).

17 Apr 73 FAA Certification granted to 747-200C.

Jun 73 First flight of 747 with CF6 engines (51,000lb thrust CF6-50D on the Boeing-owned 'prototype' aircraft).

13 Jun 73 First flight of E-4A (31676, for US Air Force, as Advanced Airborne National Command Post Aircraft).

Aug 73 Boeing announces the launch of the 747SP (Special Performance) programme.

31 Aug 73 First flight of 747SR (JA8117 for Japan Air Lines).

Sep 73 747 first proposed as Space Shuttle carrier aircraft.

Jan 74 FAA Certificate is issued for the CF6-powered 747.

Feb 74 First 747 modified to Combi standard redelivered to Sabena (OO-SGA, 747-129 fitted with rear side cargo door).

7 Mar 75 First production-line Combi delivered. (C-GAGA, 747-233B Combi to Air Canada).

4 Jul 75 First flight of the 747SP (N747SP in Boeing colours, but later to Pan Am as N530PA).

12 Nov 75 747SP begins 75,000 mile world sales tour.

4 Feb 76 FAA Certification granted to 747SP.

3 Sep 76 First flight of RR RB.211-powered 747 (G-BDXA, a 747-236B for British Airways).

18 Feb 77 First flight of Space Shuttle/747 combination (from NASA's Dryden Flight Research Center).

4 May 77 FAA Certification granted to RB.211/747 combination.

12 Jun 80 Boeing announces plans for the Stretched Upper Deck option, designated 747SUD (later to become 747-300).

21 Sep 82 Roll-out of first Stretched Upper Deck 747-300.

5 Oct 82 First flight of 747-300 (HB-IGC, a 747-357 Combi for Swissair).

4 Mar 83 FAA Certification granted to 747-300.

Early 84 Work begins on 747-300A (Advanced) — later to become the 747-400.

29 Apr 88 First flight of 747-400 — which ultimately led to the end of 747 Classic production.

Sep 90 Last 747-300 delivered (OO-SGD, a 747-329 for Sabena).

Nov 91 First flight of the final Classic 747 (JA8194, a 747-281F for Nippon Cargo Airlines.

INDEX